NES. DE SAN ANTONIO

EL BOBSEQON

EL RODEO

VARGAS

VALLECITO

LOS NARANJOS

MONJARAS

ACURA

TORO MUERTO

LOS ENCUENTROS

EL NANZAL

EL CHORRO

QDA DEL CHORRO

AYALO

LA PITA

FLORESTA

EL PO

LAS

RIO CHIQUITO

CUBEJO ABAJO

TRUJILLO

EL CIRUELO

CONCEPCION DE MARIA

CORRAL VIEJO

BO EL SAUSE

BO GUAYACASTE

JAGUA S.E.

EL CAULOTE

CONGUIRE

LA FLORETA

COYOLITO

EL PORTILLO

COYOLITO

STA MARIA DEL CARBON

PESH

AGUA BLANCA

DOS PORTILLOS

CASA QUEMADA

SAN ESTEBAN

EL TUNAL

EL OLOTE?

GUAPINOL

REVENTA

LAS MINDELAS

AGUA FRIA

SAN AGUSTIN

BLANCO MORENO

CARNEVACA

LOMA PLANA

GUAYABILLAS

EL BIJAO

EL MICO

EL ACUACATE S.E.

EL OLOTE

MAL PAIS

SIERRA DE AGALTA

N AGUSTIN
PRIETO

HECHO POR: HENRY MENCIA 2004

THEY CALL IT
PARAISO

14 Dec 2005

Mac,

You were an early part of the success of our efforts in Honduras. Thanks for all you've done for so many people ... and for being such a _great_ friend!

God Bless You,

Jerry

THEY CALL IT
PARAISO

—

SHARING GOD'S LOVE
THROUGH HONDURAS OUTREACH

—

DICK PARKER

LOOKING GLASS BOOKS

Honduras Outreach, Inc.
Decatur, Georgia
(404) 378-0919
HOI.org
Email: askhoi@hoi.org

Photography contributed by Dr. Steve Wilks, Sue Church, Bill Lisenby (silhouettes),
Kelly Holyoak, Jerry Eickhoff, Mike Dalton, Allison Per-Lee, and Beth Barnwell.

Published by
Looking Glass Books
Decatur, Georgia

Manufactured in the Canada

ISBN 1-929619-27-8

Book and jacket design by Burtch Hunter Design

To Archie B. Crenshaw,
a true man of God, who heard His call and acted upon it,
taking us to the wonderful people and beautiful land of Honduras.
Thank you for inviting us along for the journey of our lives!

———

THE HONDURAS OUTREACH BOARD OF DIRECTORS
AND NORTH AMERICAN MISSIONARIES

HONDURAS OUTREACH PARTNERS

NAME	CITY
Abundant Life Church	Greer, SC
Aely United Methodist Church	Beavercreek, OH
Agnes Scott College	Decatur, GA
Alpharetta First United Methodist Church	Alpharetta, GA
Athens-Elberton District of the United Methodist Church	Athens, GA
Atlanta Emory District of the United Methodist Church	Decatur, GA
Auburn Christian Fellowship	Auburn, AL
Austin Helps Honduras	Austin, TX
Barnesville First United Methodist Church	Barnesville, GA
Bethany United Methodist Church	Austin, TX
Bible Training Center for Church Leaders and Pastors	Atlanta, GA & Orlando, FL
Big Canoe Chapel	Big Canoe, GA
Blaine Memorial United Methodist Church	Seattle, WA
Bowen & Bowen Construction	Atlanta, GA
Broad Street Church of Christ	LaGrange, GA
Broadway Christian Church	Columbia, MO
Buford Presbyterian Church	Buford, GA
Camp Glisson of the United Methodist Church	Dahlonega, GA
Campus View Church of Christ	Athens, GA
Cannon United Methodist Church	Snellville, GA
Cedar Crest Baptist Church	West Monroe, LA
Central Baptist Church Lawrenceville	Lawrenceville, GA
Central Baptist Church Newnan	Newnan, GA
Christ by the Sea United Methodist Church	Vero Beach, FL
Christian Veterinary Mission	Seattle, WA
Church of Grace Hill	Barnesville, GA
Church of Joy	Williamson, GA
Church of the Hills Presbyterian Church	Duluth, GA
Conyers First United Methodist Church	Conyers, GA
Conyers Presbyterian Church	Conyers, GA
Cornerstone United Methodist Church	Newnan, GA
Covington United Methodist Church	Covington, GA
Davidson United Methodist Church	Davidson, NC
Decatur First United Methodist Church	Decatur, GA
Decatur Presbyterian Church	Decatur, GA
Decatur Rotary Club	Decatur, GA
DePaw University	Greencastle, IN
Dripping Springs United Methodist Church	Dripping Springs, TX
Duluth Rotary Club	Duluth, GA
Duluth United Methodist Church	Duluth, GA
East Cobb United Methodist Church	Marietta, GA
Episcopal Church of the Nativity	Dothan, AL
Farm Church	Bishop, GA

Fellowship of Believers. . . . . Barnesville, GA
First Baptist Wimberley . . . . Wimberley, TX
First Presbyterian Church of Atlanta . . . . Atlanta, GA
First Presbyterian Church of Meridian . . . . Meridian, MS
First Presbyterian of Church Grapevine . . . . Grapevine, TX
First United Methodist Church Elberton. . . . . Elberton, GA
First United Methodist Church of Kalamazoo . . . . Kalamazoo, MI
Ft. Walton Beach Church of Christ. . . . . Ft. Walton Beach, FL
Georgia State University. . . . . Atlanta, GA
General Board of Global Ministries . . . . Atlanta, GA
Gloria Dei Lutheran Church. . . . . Rochester, MN
Glenn Memorial United Methodist Church . . . . Atlanta, GA
Grace Presbyterian Church . . . . Springfield, VA
Grayson United Methodist Church . . . . Grayson, GA
Hamilton Mill United Methodist Church . . . . Dacula, GA
Hands to Honduras, N. Ga. Conference, United Methodist Church Youth Mission. . . . Atlanta, GA
Hartwell United Methodist Church . . . . Hartwell, GA
Harbor Christian Community Church . . . . Hilton Head Island, SC
Harding University. . . . . Searcy, AR
Highland Church of Christ. . . . . Montgomery, AL
Hillside United Methodist Church . . . . Woodstock, GA
Hinsdale United Methodist Church. . . . . Hinsdale, IL
Holy Trinity Episcopal Church . . . . Decatur, GA
Hope-Beckham, Inc. . . . . Atlanta, GA
Horizon Presbyterian Church. . . . . Phoenix, AZ
Kingswood United Methodist Church . . . . Dunwoody, GA
Knott Avenue Christian Church . . . . Anaheim, CA
LaGrange College . . . . LaGrange, GA
Lake Placid United Methodist Church. . . . . Lake Placid, FL
Lakeside Presbyterian Church . . . . Brandon, MS
Lawrenceville Rotary Club. . . . . Lawrenceville, GA
Liberty Hill Church . . . . Canton, GA
Memorial Drive Presbyterian Church. . . . . Houston, TX
Mission del Sol Prebyterian Church . . . . Tempe, AZ
Morningside Presbyterian Church. . . . . Atlanta, GA
Morrow United Methodist Church . . . . Morrow, GA
Mountain Park United Methodist Church. . . . . Stone Mountain, GA
Mt Bethel United Methodist Church. . . . . Marietta, GA
Mt Gilead Baptist Church. . . . . Dahlonega, GA
Mt Vernon Presbyterian Church . . . . Atlanta, GA
Nacoochee United Methodist Church . . . . Sautee-Nacoochee, GA
Newnan First Baptist Church. . . . . Newnan, GA
Northbrook United Methodist Church . . . . Roswell, GA
Northlake Rotary. . . . . Decatur, GA
Northside United Methodist Church . . . . Atlanta, GA
Northway Christian Church. . . . . Dallas, TX
Oak Hill Baptist Church . . . . Lawrenceville, GA
Pattillo Family Foundation. . . . . Decatur, GA
Pittulloch Foundation . . . . Decatur, GA
Peachtree Road United Methodist Church . . . . Atlanta, GA
Pensacola Church of Christ. . . . . Pensacola, FL

Pleasant Hill Presbyterian Church	Duluth, GA
Plymart, Inc.	Norcross, GA
Providence Presbyterian Church	Hilton Head Island, SC
Reinhart College	Waleska, GA
Riva Trace Baptist Church	Annapolis, MD
Rockdale Foundation	Conyers, GA
Royston First United Methodist Church	Royston, GA
Samford University	Birmingham, AL
Second Ponce de Leon Baptist Church	Decatur, GA
Shandon Presbyterian Church	Columbia, SC
Simpsonwood United Methodist Church	Norcross, GA
Smoke Rise Baptist Church	Stone Mountain, GA
Soccer for Souls	Tampa, FL
South Cobb Rotary	Austell, GA
South National Church of Christ	Springfield, Mo.
St James Episcopal Church	Macon, GA
St James United Methodist Church	Tampa Palms, FL
St James United Methodist Church	Augusta, GA
St. Luke's Presbyterian Church	Dunwoody, GA
St Mark United Methodist Church	Augusta, GA
St Mark United Methodist Church	Atlanta, GA
St Martin's Lutheran Church	Austin, TX
St Thomas United Methodist Church	Glen Ellyn, IL
St Timothy United Methodist Church	Stone Mountain, GA
Tabernacle Baptist Church	Cartersville, GA
Tampa YMCA	Tampa, FL
Tampa Young Life	Tampa, FL
Tarrytown United Methodist Church	Austin, TX
The Crenshaw Trust	Athens, GA
The Light Foundation	Tampa, FL
Thomson First Baptist Church	Thomson, GA
Trinity on the Hill United Methodist Church	Augusta, GA
Tuckston United Methodist Church	Athens, GA
United Methodist Church of San Marcos	San Marcos, TX
University of South Carolina	Columbia, SC
University United Methodist Church	Austin, TX
Vanderbilt University	Nashville, TN
Wake Forest University	Winston-Salem, NC
Walnut Hill United Methodist Church	Dallas, TX
Waterview Church of Christ	Richardson, TX
Wesley Memorial United Methodist Church	Opelika, AL
Wesley United Methodist Church	Evans, GA
Wesleyan Christian Schools	Norcross, GA
Westminster Presbyterian Church	Snellville, GA
Westwood United Methodist Church	Cincinnati, OH
Wimberley United Methodist Church	Wimberley, TX
Wofford College	Spartanburg, SC
World Outreach Sponsored Groups, Joe Glenn	GA, TN, CA, LA, NC, SC, IL
Zebulon United Methodist Church	Zebulon, GA

CONTENTS

BY JOHN PRATT

FOREWORD

For God so loved the world . . .
John 3:16

THE LAST roof truss was lifted into place in 1990 on the first Honduras Outreach construction project at Rancho el Paraiso, the milking barn, and the view from the peak was majestic and remarkable. Surrounded by steep mountains on every horizon, it was a view of a land much as rural North America might have looked in 1890. A rambling ranch house or hacienda was the only building with walls. Barbed-wire fences divided pastures from planted fields and narrow paths. There was no electricity or phone, and therefore no poles supporting cables or wires. There were many travelers on horse or donkey or foot, and oxen were pulling carts with gigantic wooden wheels. Bicycles and trucks were rare, and there were no cars.

The view from the same place today is familiar but startlingly different. The surrounding mountains are still as beautiful, but close by the hacienda has been joined by two dormitories, a large kitchen and dining facilities, eight duplex staff houses, a nutrition center, a seminary, a busy medical clinic, a store, a barn, a kindergarten, an elementary school, and a middle school. Buses shuttle children to and from school. There are

lots of trucks, even more bicycles, electricity, radiotelephone, and e-mail. Hundreds of homes in the valley are healthier now with concrete floors, chimneys, latrines, and gardens.

Few who visited from North America in 1990 could have imagined the changes visible today . . . but this is an interim report. This is about successes of imagination and even bigger dreams.

When my daughter Caroline went with me to Honduras for the first time at the age of seventeen, I asked her to think while she was there about what is required for a happy, successful life. That was a version of the same question every North American visitor asks: How can I possibly help here? Where should I start? What is the greatest need? Can I actually make a difference?

This book is about those questions and the answers that are coming into focus. What is required is this:

- Clean water, good health, comfortable shelter
- Successful agriculture or other sources of nutritious, plentiful food
- Infrastructure: transportation for goods and people, roads, bridges, sanitation
- Education

On these foundations a healthy economy can flourish. Add freedom of choice, assembly, worship, and speech to the capacities provided by health, nutrition, shelter and education, and mutually supportive communities flourish where people can worship God and nurture their spirituality.

We can now realistically imagine in fifteen to twenty years a prosperous Agalta Valley bisected north to south by a paved highway. A valley dotted with churches, groves of trees, high schools, clinics, comfortable homes, and productive agriculture connected to the world by e-mail, air travel, and good roads. A place in which children can even attend college and to which they want to return from colleges farther away.

What must we do to help Hondurans in the Agalta Valley and serve God?

What is needed?

What is the most important thing God's children can do?

If God made this universe and everything in it—and so loved it to give his only Son—those creations must be very important and worthy of our care.

We can pursue the salvation of creation. The salvation of God's land and waters, plants and animals, men and women, girls and boys.

We can pursue it at Rancho el Paraiso, and then we can go out from Paraiso and pursue it in the rest of the world.

Like the Bible, this is a book that begins in Paradise.

AUTHOR'S NOTE

I heard the voice of the LORD, saying: "Whom shall I send, and who will go for Us?"
Then I said, "Here am I! Send me."

Isaiah 6:8

VISIT THE home or office of almost anyone who has served the people of the Agalta Valley, and you will see a photograph, a handmade cedar cross, pottery, or other artwork—some visible reminder that, in a glance, takes the owner back to the heart of the one who is still in Honduras, back to a place of light and peace. Similarly, this book is an attempt to create a portal, through stories and photographs, to a "city on a hill" in central Honduras. As with any attempt to count the uncountable or know the unknowable, this work is in no way complete. The apostle John wrote at the end of his Gospel, "If every one of [the things Jesus did] were written down, I suppose that even the whole world would not have room for the books that would be written" (21:25, NIV). An unabridged collection of memories from the thousands of North Americans and Hondurans who have come together through Honduras Outreach would be almost as overwhelming.

CHAPTER 1

A LIGHT IN THE VALLEY

"You are the light of the world. A city on a hill cannot be hidden. Neither do people light a lamp and put it under a bowl. Instead they put it on its stand, and it gives light to everyone in the house. In the same way, let your light shine before men, that they may see your good deeds and praise your Father in heaven."

Matthew 5:14-16 (NIV)

THEY COME by the busload, North Americans committed to becoming God's light in a world of darkness. Every Sunday the bus crosses the high mountain ridge east of Juticalpa, Honduras, and rattles down the bumpy dirt road into the Agalta Valley, dragging a swirling wake of dust behind it. The people inside the bus look out the windows across the valley toward distant mountains to the south and north. *Todo es verde.* Everything is green until they come to a village, then everything is brown—the color of dried mud. Mud houses, mud yards, mud road, mud-covered animals.

When they hear the bus coming, the people of the village stop whatever they are doing to wave and smile a smile that instantly transcends the mud and dust. The people inside the bus smile, and some of them wave back. They do not yet know what the bus means to the people in the village—or what the people in the village will mean to them.

The bus rolls on, and another thin layer of dust settles on the homes, the animals, and the people.

Those who have made the trip before begin to see slight but real changes in the villages about fifty kilometers out from their destination. All of the children wear clothes. There is less litter in yards. Change appears more dramatic ten kilometers farther down the road. Someone makes note of the chimneys in the homes, and first-time visitors get a glimpse of a latrine. Near the bridge over the Rio de Mataderos, a veteran calls out, "Home Depot coming up on the right." Below the bridge on each side of the river, families have set up operations mixing sand from the river bottom with cement and water to make concrete blocks, which Honduras Outreach buys by the thousands to build homes, latrines, and schools. The families by the river

are among the many entrepreneurs taking advantage of economic opportunities created by the people on the bus.

The bus nears the village of Culuco, and from the horizon rise two of the most important indications of the visitors' impact on this valley—an elementary and a middle school, low stucco buildings with red tile roofs. On Monday morning the people on the bus will smile when they see children walking the dusty roads to school in their uniforms, bright white blouses or shirts with plaid skirts or navy slacks. They look like they could be walking to any prep school back home.

Turning right, the bus leaves the two-lane road and winds down a path through the trees, bouncing through mudholes and slowing for a child driving an ox cart.

"There's the milking barn," someone says, pointing off to the left, and the first steep roof since arriving in Honduras

reminds the visitors of the early North American influence on the valley. A moment later the bus turns left into the ranch entrance, with the medical clinic on the right, the chapel across the little road, and the dormitory for pastors-in-training beside the chapel.

To the first-time rider on the bus, all of these things—the schools, the chapel, the chimneys, the latrines, and the medical clinic—are the good deeds that Christ was talking about in the Sermon on the Mount. This place, Rancho el Paraiso, where North Americans come every week to serve Hondurans, is a city on a hill, and its light is spreading throughout the Agalta Valley.

On Monday morning, though, the people on the bus will see an unexpected light. They will enter a village and meet its people. They may be invited into a two-room mud home with pallets for sleeping, and on the wall will hang a single adornment—a

Popsicle-stick cross made by one of the family's children when the North Americans came to their village a year ago. And whether or not they speak the same language, by the end of the short week, visitors and Hondurans will have communicated love to one another. The visitors will be humbled, reflecting on an earlier expectation of bringing light to these loving people. God's light already shines through the people of the Agalta Valley. They are the salt of the earth. Someone will remember Mother Teresa's famous quotation: "In the face of every child, every leper, and every poor person we minister to, I see the face of Christ and experience His blessings."

Honduras is one of the poorest countries in the Western Hemisphere, and the Agalta Valley is one of the poorest areas of Honduras. A Honduran family's entire worldly goods might fit

into a single North American closet. Still, the people reach out
to give, not to receive. They offer love, joy, and kindness in
their hospitality. They show us how to live patiently, waiting for
the seasons to provide what they need. Even the youngest
among them model faithfulness in their loyalty to one
another. All of these gifts of the Spirit and more, they
generously share with us. They see us as the stranger
and invite us in. In them we see the face of Christ
and are overwhelmed by it.

We climbed onto a plane and then a bus for a
journey to the center of Honduras, and our journey
took us into the heart of another person. We toiled
and sweat alongside our new brothers and sisters,
covering dirt floors with concrete, venting smoke from
homes with new chimneys, and keeping water sources

cleaner by building latrines alongside homes. We taught their children Bible stories and sang with them about the love of Christ. We expected to give, but we received far more. We received an outpouring of gratitude from parents who know their children are less likely to become ill from parasites. We received hugs from children who stayed close by all week and reached up for our hand as we walked through the village. And we experienced the peace that passes all understanding while we lived among the people in this place.

CHAPTER 2

PARADISE

"As the Father has sent Me, I also send you."

John 20:21

NORTH AMERICANS call it the ranch. Hondurans call it *Paraiso*. Paradise.

Decades before Honduras Outreach established a mission in the Agalta Valley, Rancho el Paraiso was already there. In 1887 the great-grandparents of José Aguilla, a present-day judge in nearby San Esteban, built a hacienda in the valley, and for most of the next hundred years, cattle grazed on the surrounding sixteen hundred acres. Rancho el Paraiso (pronounced pah-rah-EE-soh) became known as one of the most prosperous cattle operations in the department (state) of Olancho.

Olancho, the largest of the country's eighteen departments, earned a reputation as the Wild West of Honduras. For generations the mountainous central region of the country was virtually ignored by the Honduran government. Left to govern and take care of themselves, the people often resorted

to violence and intimidation. Naturalist Archie Carr lived in Olancho during the mid-twentieth century and wrote of it in his book *High Jungles and Low*:

Hardly anyone goes out there . . . but everyone is conscious of the place and that aura of mystery and promise about it, and everywhere you hear that it has more future than any major area in Central America. . . . [Olancho is] a land of great diversity and great contrasts, a frontier . . . with the blood of the first wave of conquistadores in its people and men still wild along its lowland streams.

Carr was fascinated by the people of Olancho, and he came to love them. "The patience and the endurance of the poor mountain people are displayed in the amazing journeys which they make on foot," he wrote. "The sheer doggedness exhibited on these trips always moves me."

Archie Carr left Honduras in 1949, and three decades later there were still many areas in Olancho where almost nothing had changed. The region was still isolated by a lack of roads, largely ignored by government, and populated by poor but determined people. Only in small cities like Catacamas, Juticalpa, and San Esteban was there any hope of education, and even there almost no one attended school beyond third grade.

Sabel Guifarro was among the economically privileged few in Catacamas. His mother, Naomi, owned a city block in Catacamas, a city of thirty-six thousand, and rented out several stores. Sabel finished high school and went to the United States to attend college at the University of Southwestern Louisiana. There he was assigned a dorm room with Rick Machen, a freshman from Slidell, Louisiana.

A year earlier Rick, his brother Ken, and their cousin had participated in a Church of Christ mission trip to Switzerland and returned with a passion for Christ and world evangelism. Rick's father, Richard, seeing the transformations of the boys, decided that he would one day lead an international mission trip—but to somewhere closer and less expensive than Switzerland. Richard studied a map of Central America and dreamed of the opportunities that might lie there.

Cattle made Olancho wealthy and kept it isolated. The good pasturage lay on terrace plains as remote from centers of civilization as any part of Middle America, and the haciendas quickly became self-sufficient.

Archie Carr
High Jungles and Low

Rick came home from college one weekend and brought Sabel with him. In fact, every weekend that Rick came home, Sabel joined him. The Machen house, sitting on thirty acres at the edge of Bayou Bonfouca, was a magnet for friends when the kids were growing up, and it remained so through their college years.

Richard Machen and his wife, Louise, extended their hospitality further when Sabel's sister was diagnosed with cancer. She was brought to New Orleans for treatment, and the Machens let the Guifarros stay in their house on Lake Pontchartrain during her two-month recovery. Louise was coteaching a Bible study and introduced Sabel to a relationship with Christ. Sabel asked Louise to teach the Bible to his family—he had to translate into Spanish—and they all committed their lives to Christ.

The following summer, 1980, Naomi Guifarro invited the Machens to come to Honduras and bring friends who would

help them share the gospel in Catacamas. Without even seeking an opportunity, except through prayer, Richard's dream of an international mission trip was becoming reality.

Richard and Louise recruited twenty-five people for their first mission trip. "We're a bunch of greenhorns," Richard told a friend, "and we don't know what we are doing, but God does." One member of the group recruited a young Mexican, Israel Flores, to do the preaching.

As they neared their departure date, several members of the group had not yet come up with enough money to pay for their trip. Rather than risk losing them, Richard and Louise offered to reach into their savings to pay their way. As soon as they made that commitment, financial opportunities opened for those lacking funds, and by their departure date they all had raised enough money.

A CALL IS HEARD

When the group arrived in Catacamas, Naomi took them to El Sembrador, a ranch and school just outside the city, founded by a missionary family from Ohio in 1954.

"It was such an impressive operation," Richard recalls. "They did a wonderful job of training and educating the young men who were selected to live on the ranch."

Richard's vision of leading international mission trips began to broaden when he saw the positive impact of El Sembrador on the young men and their families, and he considered the possibility of a permanent outpost—a place for Hondurans and Christian missionaries and teachers to come together.

"Who knows when a dream is born?" he says. "I would have to say it happened at El Sembrador."

The dream of a ranch may have been born in 1980, but it would be five years before God seemed to move on it. In the meantime, the Machens continued to take people on mission trips to Honduras. While in Catacamas in 1985, Richard, his friend Jack Odum, and two others borrowed a Jeep to drive to the north coast town of Trujillo purely as an adventure. The road hadn't been scraped through several rainy seasons, and though it was dry that day, the ruts were so wide and the holes so deep, their choices were to drive ten miles per hour all the way to their destination or to rattle all their bones loose. They bumped along slowly, and when they stopped for a break, one of Richard's companions, exhausted and frustrated, fell out onto the road flat on his back, and cried, "Lord, tell me what I did to deserve this, and I will never do it again!" When they resumed their trek, Richard told himself, "Never again as long as I live will I travel this road."

Then they reached the valley near San Esteban, and the beauty of it—green hills and waterfalls cascading off the sides of mountains—took their breath away. Richard felt the Holy Spirit moving within him, and he knew that this was the place God would bring an international mission to reality.

For two more years Richard carried the dream—and the call to create a mission based on the model of El Sembrador—in his heart. Whenever he took groups to Catacamas, he discovered more about the people and the villages in the Agalta Valley outside San Esteban. In 1987 he took four other men on a trip down the "never again" road and parked at the town square in San Esteban. A storekeeper stood at his front door, and Richard asked Wayne Gaines, one of his companions who spoke Spanish, to ask the man if he knew anybody with a ranch for sale in the valley.

"See the lady sitting in her car with her two daughters?" the storekeeper asked.

"Yes," Wayne answered.

"Her husband just died, and she wants to sell their ranch."

Wayne quickly translated for Richard.

"You're kidding!" Richard said.

"That's what he says."

"Well, let's go ask."

The five gringos walked over to the car and, sure enough, the woman, Rosemary de Diaz, said she wanted to sell her ranch—Rancho el Paraiso. She told the men to follow her; she would lead them there.

They followed her truck west out of San Esteban and turned off the main road onto an even bumpier trail, but didn't have to travel far before they arrived at an old clay-tiled house that looked like it belonged on the Ponderosa on the TV show *Bonanza.* The woman showed them into the house, which had a wood floor and high ceilings. Wayne translated her explanation that there was a

hand-dug well for water and an outhouse in back. A milking barn
next to the house doubled as a storage shed for saddles and grain.

The men borrowed horses to ride out to survey the spread—
more than six miles around—and Richard knew this was the
place God had in mind. They rode back to the hacienda, and
within a few hours he and the widow had agreed to a price.

Richard didn't explain to Señora de Diaz that he didn't
have the money. She might not understand or appreciate his
reliance on God's provision. As he considered the ways God
might provide the necessary capital, he thought of Joe Glenn,
president of World Outreach Foundation.

World Outreach had been founded by Archie Crenshaw, a
former Church of Christ minister who had begun building
high-rise apartment buildings for the elderly and committing a
large percentage of the proceeds to the foundation, which had
supported missions around the world.

CHAPTER 3

THE CHILDREN

"The Spirit of the Lord God is upon Me, because the LORD has anointed Me to preach good tidings to the poor; He has sent Me to heal the brokenhearted."

Isaiah 61:1

RICHARD MACHEN had no idea when he called Joe Glenn that Joe had only recently returned from Honduras. Catacamas, in fact. A friend had invited Archie Crenshaw to join a group visiting Escuela Biblica, a school in Catacamas for training pastors of rural churches founded by the Church of Christ. But Archie could not get away from work, so he asked Joe to go in his place.

Archie believed his daughters might benefit by a visit to a developing nation as well, and his two younger girls, Cissy and Candy, seized the opportunity to experience a week in another culture. Cissy was in college and Candy had recently graduated with a degree in health education from Pepperdine University. They joined Joe and twenty or so others, many of them members of the Escuela Biblica board.

When they arrived in Catacamas, the girls' first impression was of the children. Everywhere they looked they saw children running and playing.

They asked why the children weren't in school and learned a lesson in Honduran economics. Families could not afford to send their children to school because the children needed uniforms and textbooks, which they had to buy. In a subsistence economy, many families didn't have money for those things.

Cissy and Candy visited villages around Catacamas in the rural state of Olancho where there was no running water and met sick children who had never seen a doctor in their lives. Late one afternoon the wife of one of the Escuela Biblica students brought her infant to Catacamas looking for medical help.

The baby was dying of dehydration. She had terrible diarrhea, and her mother said she had had it for several days. A nurse in the local clinic had told the mother a few days earlier what to do for her daughter, but when the infant didn't improve, the mother went back to the "old way," which is to stop giving the child liquid. No water in, no diarrhea out, she believed.

A Guatemalan health care professional who had married a North American was traveling with the Church of Christ group and immediately recognized the problem. She lightly pinched the baby's skin, which was so dry that it stayed in that position. She sent someone to the pharmacy with money and instructions to buy the necessary ingredients to rehydrate the child.

Forty-five minutes after receiving the treatment, the child looked as normal as any other baby. To the North Americans, who had never seen such severe dehydration, the simple treatment had been like a miracle. They also wondered how many children were not being treated for such simple but deadly conditions.

The board of Escuela Biblica held a meeting before leaving the country, where they agreed, "It's sinful for us to graduate these young men and send them back up to preach in villages

where there is absolutely no medical help at all. They won't even know how to stop something as simple as diarrhea. God's only Son was a medical missionary who came and healed and reconciled people to God. Why can't we do the same thing with these people?" So they hired a nurse in Catacamas to teach public health training to all the ministry students.

Joe Glenn believes God sent that sick baby to Catacamas that day, because the events she set in motion have changed an entire way of life in Olancho, Honduras.

When he returned to the United States, Joe told his church in Decatur, Georgia, what he had experienced. Sitting in the congregation was Dr. Robert Clark, a former navy doctor who had tropical disease training and had served in Guatemala. Dr. Clark was so moved by Joe's impressions of Honduras that he immediately made arrangements to move to the country with his wife and children.

We are drawn to the children—the Honduran children whose dark eyes sparkle with joy and hope.

The vision of Honduras Outreach began when a North American adult looked into the eyes of a Honduran child and experienced the love and compassion that come only from God. And at every critical moment leading to the establishment of this ministry, there stood a child.

Within a year Dr. Clark had organized PrediSan—which, like Escuela Biblica, was supported by the Church of Christ—to teach basic health care principles and techniques to community health volunteers in Catacamas. The name PrediSan is the combination of the Spanish words for *preach* and *heal,* and is inspired by Luke 9:2, where Jesus sends his disciples out "to preach the kingdom of God and to heal the sick."

Cissy and Candy Crenshaw also went to work to help the children of Honduras. They told friends and family what they had seen, and a member of their church donated cloth for school uniforms. Others gave money to help buy books and fund a school, and soon they had raised enough to start the School of the Good Samaritan with thirty children in first grade. The following year they had enough money to add a second grade, and soon a North American church adopted the school in its mission effort. Archie responded to his daughters' enthusiasm by funding numerous scholarships for the schoolchildren in Catacamas.

In the weeks after he returned, Joe brainstormed with Archie and others about ways World Outreach Foundation might help more directly in Honduras. As if the timing were divinely ordained, at about the same time, Richard Machen, whom Joe knew through the Church of Christ, called from Louisiana and asked if he could meet with Archie and him to discuss an idea for a mission.

Richard and Jack Odum flew to Atlanta to make their pitch over lunch with Archie and Joe. Archie got tied up with business and arrived late, but then he started to talk. "As soon as he took a breath," Richard recalls, "we made our pitch, and we didn't stop to take a breath. We were scared he would start to talk again."

Archie's heart for rural Honduras had already been softened by the stories Candy, Cissy, and Joe had told him. Richard added his own experiences, then asked, "Wouldn't it be nice if we had a ranch down in Olancho? We could help with health care, create summer youth programs for Americans, and get college students to come down in summers and help out."

Archie thought that sounded like a good idea.

As it so happened, Richard said, there was just such a ranch for sale. He described Rancho el Paraiso and explained that if World Outreach would make the down payment of $75,000, his organization would sell the horses and cattle on the ranch and pay back the money. Then they would raise enough additional money through donations to make monthly payments from that point forward.

Archie liked the idea and said he would get back with an answer shortly, but Richard and Jack pressed for an answer right away. "We'll get back with you soon," Archie said.

Richard and Jack returned to Louisiana. Archie and Joe prayed about Richard's proposal for several days, then decided World Outreach would make the $75,000 loan, which they saw

as a gift, because they were skeptical that Richard's business model would generate enough revenue to repay. "It's God's money," Archie said. "Let's give it a shot." Their only stipulation was that Joe be placed on the board governing the ranch.

That requirement fulfilled, the down payment was made. The sale of the horses and cattle netted only $30,000, however, and the hacienda needed improvements so the Machens could bring youth groups down the following summer. Archie and Joe allowed Richard to delay repayment, and the century-old hacienda underwent major repairs. Jack Odum and others built a water tank and a septic system for the hacienda and converted an old stable to bunk rooms.

The following month, the ranch made its first $4,000 note payment to Señora de Diaz in San Esteban, but when the second monthly payment came due, there was no money in the bank. Richard called Archie, and World Outreach made the payment. Otherwise they would have lost their $75,000 and the ranch. The phone calls kept coming, and World Outreach made the note payment the next month and the next and the next.

Summer was coming, and Richard had lined up youth groups to go to Rancho el Paraiso and work in nearby villages pouring concrete floors and building latrines. They needed transportation, so Richard found someone back home willing to donate an old Ford van. He didn't have the resources to ship the van to Honduras, so he and Louise decided to drive it to Mexico City, about fifteen hundred miles, where another man would meet them and drive the van to the ranch, another nine hundred miles. They recruited a Latin American friend of their son's to help them drive to Mexico City, but he almost bailed out on them when they reached the Mexico border and he realized Richard and Louise spoke no Spanish. They made the drive without incident, however, and a few days later, the ranch had a van.

Eighty North American youth visited the ranch during the summer of 1988. Donations from a Church of Christ congregation in LaGrange, Georgia, led to the building of a church across the road from the hacienda, and the Honduran pastor they recruited baptized thirteen of his neighbors down at the river La Orilla. Later in the year an orphanage was built just down the road from the church.

AS Archie's investment in Rancho el Paraiso grew, his daughters were telling him, "Daddy, you've got to go to Honduras and see it. You sent us down there with a backpack and a Swiss army knife, but you've never gone yourself. You've got to go."

Finally, in a weak moment, Archie said, "Okay, I'll go," and he instantly regretted it. He had more than he could manage in his business and not enough time to leave the country for several days. But he had given his word, so he had to go. And he believed that somehow God was in this; He wanted Archie to go to Honduras.

Archie asked Joe Glenn to go with him, but he wanted another viewpoint from someone outside of World Outreach. He called his friend Jerry Eickhoff and asked him to go along.

CHAPTER 4

TREASURES IN HEAVEN

Jesus . . . said to him, "One thing you lack: Go your way, sell whatever you have and give to the poor . . . and come, take up the cross, and follow Me."

Mark 10:21

ARCHIE COULDN'T have picked a worse time to call Jerry Eickhoff. Or a better one.

Like the young ruler who asked Jesus what he could do to inherit eternal life, Jerry had "kept the commandments from his youth." He had grown up in the church and sincerely committed his life to Christ. Like the young ruler, Jerry had been successful in business. In 1986 the company he cofounded, Bank Earnings International (BEI), went public, and for the next year it continued to grow. Balancing his commitments to his faith, his family, and his business grew difficult for Jerry when the company and the market demanded more than just his time. It occupied his thoughts even when he was at home or sitting in the pew.

Then on October 19, 1987, the worst day in stock market history to that point, Jerry experienced firsthand the meaning of treasure "that

moth or rust destroys." On that black Monday he was sitting in a meeting in Dallas trying to keep his eye off the electronic stock market ticker across the room, but every time BEI tracked across the screen, he added up his losses into the millions. The company was never in danger of financial collapse, but the drop in value had a huge negative effect on shareholders.

Jerry was sitting at his desk working through those problems in the fall of 1988 when Archie Crenshaw called. Archie had been Jerry's college baseball coach, mentor, and a Christian model for more than two decades. He was also an excellent businessman. Archie didn't call often, but when he did, Jerry stopped what he was doing and listened.

"I'm going to Honduras to a little Christian mission down there in a couple of weeks," Archie said. "I don't know where it is, and I don't want to go, and I sure as shootin' don't want to go by myself. Will you go with me?"

Jerry didn't have time for a trip to Honduras. And like Archie, he didn't want to go. He had a financial ship to right. In the moment Archie asked, however, Jerry didn't think of those things. He still isn't sure why, but without even calling Jean, his wife, he told Archie, "Sure, I'll go."

RICHARD Machen told Archie, Jerry, and Joe Glenn that they would be shocked by the destitution they would see in Honduras. He tried to soften the impact by creatively managing their itinerary; rather than fly into the capital city, Tegucigalpa, where poverty appeared overwhelming, Richard had them join him, his wife, and son Ken on a flight from New Orleans to Roatán, in the Bay Islands.

Roatán may have been upscale by Honduran standards, but Archie and Jerry were not used to chickens and pigs roaming freely right outside the door and filthy children begging at every corner. And their bug-infested room did not make for a restful night. "This place is an abomination," Archie told Jerry as they turned the lights out.

The next morning Richard showed them around the city, and they ran into a group from North Carolina who were in Honduras on a medical mission. The North Carolina group included an optometrist, a dentist, and a physician who had shipped their equipment down in advance on a military transport plane. Because of a crisis in Panama, the planes were diverted to that country instead. So they went to the local medical clinic empty-handed and did what they could with the equipment on hand, including treating a man whose arm had been cut off in a fight. The optometrist said he was pulling teeth. "I hope they're eyeteeth," Jerry said.

Richard took his group back to the airport, where they boarded a DC-3 to fly fifty miles over the emerald Caribbean to Trujillo, on the north coast of Honduras. Richard explained that Martín (pronounced mar–TEEN) Murcia, an employee at Rancho el Paraiso, would meet them at the airstrip with the Ford van that Richard had bought in Louisiana. The plane landed on

time, and when the seven Americans climbed down with their duffel bags, there was no van and no Martín. The pilot took off, and as the sound of the engine faded, Jerry, Archie, Joe, and their companions stood with their bags in the absolute quiet of the Honduran countryside. Then Louise (Richard's wife) told them it was a good thing it was still early in the day. They wouldn't want to be alone in the dark because of the banditos.

Richard did not appear concerned. They were close to town, and he suggested they all walk over to the road to catch a ride into Trujillo, where he had started a door-making business. They could wait there for Martín. The driver of a beat-up pickup truck stopped and invited the seven North Americans to jump on, and they bumped along into town. Richard told the driver where his business was, and he dropped them off at the front door. Shortly after noon, Martín and his assistant, Augustine, arrived and explained that they were late because the brakes weren't working on the van. They found a shade-tree mechanic to fix the brakes while Richard and Martín led the group to a restaurant for lunch.

The noonday sun cast severe shadows on the narrow, dusty streets, but the clear blue sky and a cool breeze off the Caribbean felt like the Holy Spirit blowing afresh through Trujillo. Richard opened a door for the group to step into a tiny

restaurant that was so dark inside they almost ran into each other. As their eyes adjusted, they realized the power was off. The proprietor invited them in anyway and explained to Martín that there was no problem. He built a little fire on the sidewalk and cooked lunch for them.

It would be several more hours before the van was repaired, so Richard showed them the city, which spooked Jerry. Around every corner stood a Honduran soldier, giving an unnerving face to the headlines in the United States. Just a few weeks earlier, Nicaraguan Sandinistas had crossed the border into rural Honduras, about sixty miles southeast of Rancho el Paraiso, in search of counterrevolutionaries, known as Contras. The Contras were at war with Sandinista leader and Nicaraguan President Daniel Ortega. Throughout the war the Contras maintained bases in Honduras from which they attacked the Nicaraguan National Guard.

When Richard and the group returned to the door factory, Martín left to check on the van. Finally, at 5:30 p.m., he drove up. Everybody loaded in and Martín drove south toward Rancho el Paraiso, about one hundred twenty kilometers away. The first few miles of the road had more potholes than pavement, and

the rest of the way, Richard said, was the dirt road he had vowed never to travel again in his life.

With no power lines beyond Trujillo, night fell quickly on the countryside. Through the darkness they watched flickering fires of huts off in the distance. In the pounding, deafening rattle of the van, Jerry gazed out the window at the fires and the stars. The constellations over Honduras are the same ones Jerry had grown up seeing from north Georgia: Orion, the Big and Little Dipper, and all the rest, although they appeared lower in the north from thirteen hundred miles closer to the equator. In the northeastern sky the Big Dipper hung upside down pointing the way toward Polaris, the North Star—the way home—barely visible above the distant northern horizon.

GOD was giving Jerry a new view of the world. He might have lost a lot of money, and he might have been having some major financial challenges, but God was showing him what truly mattered.

Hardly anyone spoke for miles. They all were exhausted, and they had to shout to be heard. Suddenly the window beside Jerry exploded, sending shards of glass all over him and filling the inside of the van. The passengers and driver all fell to the floor of the van to avoid being shot, and Martín hit the accelerator and roared down the road. When he finally felt safe enough to stop, Martín pulled off the road. He and Augustine inspected the van for bullet holes while Louise Machen pulled glass shards from Jerry's face and neck and lightly touched the blood with a handkerchief.

Martín and Augustine couldn't find any bullet holes in the side of the van, so they decided that the constant rattling had caused the window to shatter. Martín started off again, and hardly a word was spoken for miles as the travelers drifted in and out of their thoughts and prayers. Then sometime around midnight the van slammed to a dead stop in the middle of the road. Martín and Augustine got out again to survey the situation, then came back and explained that the rear end had fallen out of the van. It wouldn't go any farther.

Jerry reached back and touched his neck as everybody climbed out of the van. Archie asked, "Where do you think we are?"

"I don't know," Jerry said, "but I do know that we haven't seen another vehicle for hours, Sandinistas are just over the border, and banditos are all over the place." He took out his wallet and hid it under a rock.

O LORD, our LORD, how excellent is Your name in all the earth, who have set Your glory above the heavens! . . . When I consider Your heavens, the work of Your fingers, the moon and the stars, which You have ordained, what is man that You are mindful of him, and the son of man that You visit him?

Psalm 8:1, 3–4

Archie looked at his watch, not particularly expensive but worth a year's pay in Honduras. And he thought about Louise. How safe was she?

Martín and Ken Machen, who had been a long-distance runner in high school, stood off to one side talking with Richard, then came back and said they were close enough to the ranch for the two of them to set out on foot, hoping for a ride. The North Americans and Augustine waited in silence under the stars.

No one remembers exactly how long they sat by the road before they saw yellow headlights in the distance. As the vehicle approached, Augustine stood and waved. The big open truck pulled over and stopped, and Augustine spoke to the driver, then motioned for the Americans to climb onto the back.

Archie looked in the cab and saw three rough-looking Hondurans. He hesitated, then decided he'd rather be moving than sitting. They threw their duffel bags on top of a load of bags of coffee—at least, they said it was coffee—and climbed up on the back.

The four Americans sat on the coffee, facing backward, and looked for Ken and Martín as the truck bumped and banged across the Honduran countryside. The night grew somehow even darker, then it started to rain. Not North American-style summer rain but drenching, flood-making, pouring-down, tropical rain. The driver slowed to keep from sliding off the instantly muddy road.

An hour later the rain stopped as the truck pulled into San Esteban, which Richard explained was the closest large town to the ranch. By "large" he meant a few hundred people and electricity. The driver pulled the truck over and cut off the engine. Augustine knocked on the back window and said he thought they were going on down the road and could drop

them off at the ranch, another fifteen kilometers away. The dry
men in the cab explained that they were stopping for a beer.

So the wet Americans got down from the truck, and
Richard gave his guests a muddy walking tour of San Esteban
in the dark, always staying within sight of the truck. He pointed
to the pool hall, another bar, the church, and city hall, where
there was a telephone that sometimes worked. Finally the men
came out of the bar, so they loaded back on and rode on
toward the ranch.

Nobody said anything about Ken and Martín; they couldn't
have come this far without a ride. The truck bumped along until
Augustine knocked on the back window and told the men to
stop. A one-lane road turned off the main road. "We're here,"
Richard said.

The entrance to Rancho el Paraiso drops sharply from the
main dirt road, but in those days the drop was even steeper and
the driveway even lower, taking it down to the lowest part of the
property. The storm had turned it into a mudbath.

A flatbed truck was slipping and sliding, trying to get up the hill. When the group jumped off the coffee truck, Martín and Ken climbed out of the cab of the flatbed, and there was laughter for the first time in hours. Ken explained that they had gotten a ride back to the ranch earlier in the night and were taking the other ranch vehicle back to get the rest of the group, but they never made it up the slick hill to the main road.

Archie, Joe, Jerry, and the Machens threw their bags onto the back of the flatbed and climbed up to ride the last little bit to the ranch, but Augustine had trouble getting the truck turned around in the mud. When he finally got going in the right direction, he started fishtailing and grinding the gears. With nothing to hold on to but each other, the passengers in the back rolled from one side to another until finally the wheels started spinning and the truck stood still. They weren't riding any farther.

"Where's the ranch?" Jerry asked.

"About three hundred yards down the road," Richard said.

"Then let's go."

So they grabbed their bags and jumped off the truck, landing in foot-deep mud. Every time they lifted a foot, the mud threatened to pull their boots off.

They walked silently toward a few dim lights and the sound of a generator chugging. "That's the hacienda," Richard said. "I'm sorry we don't have a shower to clean up." A few minutes later they were greeted on the porch by Robert and Amy Machen, Richard's other son and daughter-in-law, who were at the ranch hosting several other North Americans. Jerry and Archie looked at each other under the bare bulb, both of them muddy and exhausted, Jerry with blood on his face, neck, and arms. Archie was so angry he couldn't speak. Not only had he come on this crazy trip, he had brought Jerry along with him, and right now he wasn't sure they would ever get out again.

Then Jerry said, "Archie, you said God told you to come to Honduras. Now think real carefully and tell me again exactly

what you heard. Are you sure He said *Honduras*? Maybe He said, 'Archie, get a *Honda*,' or 'Archie, go to *Honolulu*.' Could you have messed this thing up?" Finally Archie managed a smile.

Then the smell of sausage, eggs, and toast drifted out from the hacienda, and they knew better times were ahead. The ranch staff had waited up for the Americans, and a Honduran cook had started preparing food when she heard them coming. After getting something to eat, they began to feel better about the situation.

As they ate, several young North Americans came in and introduced themselves. A hydroelectric engineer from California had brought a friend with him to work on the ranch, and five youth leaders were there making plans for bringing kids down the following summer. Archie listened to their dreams, and his anger began to rise again when he imagined his own children enduring the trip he had just made. The youth leaders went on, and finally he had heard enough.

He stood up and said, "We just came within an inch of our lives getting here, and you're talking about bringing people's children down for a week at a time? You're out of your cotton-picking minds! You can't bring kids down here. You've got no telephone for fifteen miles. You don't have running water. You're not talking about some Hi-Y camp in Colorado. This isn't some FCA deal. This is a third-world country. Not to mention a war is going on right over the border. Suppose somebody breaks a leg? What are you going to do then?"

The youth ministers didn't back down, and Jerry and Archie went to bed thinking they were somewhere in the middle of Central America with a bunch of crazy people. The generator was shut off, and the ranch went silent and black.

WHEN they woke up, the sun was rising from behind the Sierra de Agalta Mountains several miles to the southeast. Jerry and Archie stepped outside the hacienda and saw Rancho el Paraiso for the first time, and they were stunned by its beauty. Century-old hardwoods reached out a hundred feet in every direction— limbs covered with orchids and bromeliads blooming in fuchsia, bright pink, and purple. Up on a hill to the west, cattle grazed quietly, and down to the east the land flattened out toward a river they could hear tumbling through the quiet morning. Martín showed Joe and them the road down to the river for bathing, and they came to breakfast cold but clean.

After breakfast Jerry and Archie walked over to a cattle corral just outside the gate where a cowboy was milking a Brahma cow with her legs tied together, and a couple of cowboys were bringing more cattle. A dozen or more Honduran children in filthy T-shirts had gathered, all of them looking malnourished, and some with distended bellies from para-sites. Each of the children held a little plastic bottle with the top cut off by a machete, watching intently as the cowboy squirted milk into a dirty bucket.

After a few minutes, one of the children stepped up, and the cowboy picked up a ladle from the manure on the ground, dipped some milk out of the bucket, and poured it into the child's bottle.

The cowboy put his ladle down in the mud again, and the boy walked away smiling broadly, carrying his milk as carefully as if it were liquid gold.

In that moment Jerry was changed. Since childhood he had heard and read Christ's words, "Blessed are the poor in spirit."

Now, for the first time, he understood. He saw the poor—the *truly* poor, the starving poor. Looking at their muddy little faces and their clear brown eyes, he believed God had a blessing for them in this world. And somehow through this ranch, God wanted Jerry to participate in that blessing.

None of the Honduran adults understood the relationship between the ladle lying in the manure and sick and dying children. Somebody had to teach them how to be more sanitary—the basics of good health and nutrition. Jerry knew people back in the States who could do those things.

Back at the hacienda, Jerry borrowed a guitar from one of the North American youth and strummed a few songs. Honduran children gathered around, and one little girl stood especially close. Jerry put down the guitar, and she sat in his lap. The child had impetigo, and Jerry asked Richard if he had any Neosporin. Watching as Jerry put medicine on the little girl's

Jesus said, "Let the little children come to Me, and do not forbid them; for of such is the kingdom of heaven."

Matthew 19:14

sores, Archie prayed, "Lord, you've got Jerry."

Later that evening as they lay on their beds in the dark, Jerry told Archie, "I've been brought down here to see how the real world is. You know, I could lose everything and still be able to find a decent meal back home. Even the homeless people in Atlanta, if they want a bathroom, can find a bathroom. If they need a meal, they can find a meal. But these children don't have anything but filthy milk. We've got to do something about it."

RICHARD Machen had business to attend to back in Trujillo, so he left the ranch after a couple of days. At the end of their visit, Richard's family would accompany Jerry, Archie, and Joe on the

public bus that would take them to the airport in La Ceiba, four hours away. Rain started as Augustine took them up to the main road on the flatbed truck, and Jerry took a final look back at the muddy corral where the children had come for milk. He knew he would be back. The tires spun as Augustine gunned the accelerator. This time he was able to get up to the main road.

After a short wait a twenty-passenger bus with *El Negro*—the Black One—painted on the side stopped, and the door opened for the six passengers. The driver was dressed in army fatigues and spoke no English. A few locals sat and leaned their heads sleepily against the windows. The North Americans dragged their duffel bags to the back of the bus as the driver hit the accelerator, and they bounced into their seats.

It was Sunday, and as they passed through the many villages along the way, they saw Honduran women walking through the mud to church with old umbrellas or parasols in a vain attempt to stay dry. Driving into the mountains, the tires began to skid. Although Jerry, Joe, and Archie laughed about it, the trip into the country had been so harrowing, they wondered aloud about Honduran public transportation. Archie called out, "El Negro, are we going to make it?"

The driver understood the question, turned around, and with a glint in his eye said, "Chocolate!" (He actually said, "¡Choh-koh-LAH-teh!")

Ken Machen, knowing the routine, reached into a backpack, pulled out a candy bar, and tossed it to him. The driver turned around, gripped the steering wheel tightly, and fishtailed up and over the summit.

Several miles farther down the road the bus again began to skid, and again the call came, this time with greater doubt, "El Negro, how are we going to make it over this one?"

The driver reached under his seat and pulled out a rope, then turned around and answered, "Gringos!"

The men instantly knew what he meant and began looking at one another to see who would answer the call. Everybody got a turn. El Negro tied the rope to the front bumper, and the gringos pulled the bus to the top of the mountain.

When Richard Machen later heard about the trip to the airport, he knew it was the last straw. The trip had been a disaster from the start. Every attempt to make a positive impression on Archie, Joe, and Jerry had failed miserably. At this point, he thought, only the Holy Spirit could soften their hearts and lead them to continue their commitment to the ranch.

CHAPTER 5

OVERCOMING FEAR

As they followed they were afraid.

Mark 10:32

BY THE TIME Jerry Eickhoff arrived home in Decatur, he had planned the summer vacation of a lifetime for his family. He wanted Jean and their children to see what he had seen as soon as possible. Jean listened as Jerry described the Honduran military, broken-down vehicles, tropical rains, outhouses, beans and rice three meals a day from a questionable kitchen, a hand-dug well, and a river for bathing—among some of the world's poorest people. She was afraid for herself, and much more for their three children. How could she protect them in that environment?

Jean, who had an intimate relationship with Christ, thought she had long ago put Kim, Kelly, and Brent in God's hands for protection. Now she was being called to trust Him in a new way.

Jerry made arrangements with Richard Machen to go to the ranch at the same time as a Church of Christ youth group from Florida. They arrived at the La Ceiba airport on Saturday afternoon

and met Martín, who directed them and the youth group to an El Negro bus. As before, the driver wore military fatigues and spoke no English.

They drove out of the city and into the countryside as the sun dropped toward the mountains. Not far from town, the driver stopped and let two openly armed men dressed in fatigues board the bus. Jean pulled Brent close to her as the two men searched the bus for Sandinista rebels. Jean's fears had become like giants, and in comparison, she and her family looked like grasshoppers. The military men found no rebels and left, and the bus bounced along into the night. The bus was boarded several more times by armed militia before arriving at the entrance to the ranch sometime after midnight. Martín led them to the hacienda, where they were greeted by Robert and Amy Machen. The

Eickhoffs had a room to themselves, and the youth group spread out in the other rooms.

Jerry had described to Jean what she would see when the sun rose: the beauty of the landscape and the poverty among the people. When dawn came, there was a comforting familiarity to the setting, even in its remoteness. The sun silhouetting the mountains to the east was the same sun that shone back home. The rolling hills dotted with grazing cattle weren't so different from those in north Georgia. Jean was experiencing the truth of Psalm 139:9–10: "If I take the wings of the morning, and dwell in the uttermost parts of the sea, even there Your hand shall lead me, and Your right hand shall hold me."

After breakfast Martín took the youth and the Eickhoffs to San Martín, where Jerry, Jean, and their daughters, Kelly and Kim, hauled water up from a river to make cement for floors while Brent played with the local children. The men of the village, with guns on their belts, sat around watching and pointing as the gringos worked. Some of the Honduran women smiled and helped. Others meandered around the village, carrying a heavy load of sadness. Many of the youngest children who could walk were naked and had distended bellies.

In her prayers Jean asked, "Lord, where do you even begin in a place like this? It's overwhelming."

She knew they had to do something, whether she was excited about it or not. God had brought

"Who among you fears the LORD? Who obeys the voice of His Servant? Who walks in darkness and has no light? Let him trust in the name of the LORD and rely upon his God."

Isaiah 50:10

them to this place, opened their eyes to poverty, and told them, *This is a place that needs help. Now what are you going to do about it?* Jean wasn't looking for that kind of mission work. She was wrapped up in her family. Jerry was wrapped up in running his company. God was stirring in them, forcing them to look beyond themselves and figure out how they could genuinely help others. Jerry believed the best way to help would be to bring a group of friends down and build a milking barn so the children could have clean, safe milk. At least that would be a first step.

THE VISION GROWS

Archie and Joe also planned a second trip to Honduras in 1989. Before they went down, Archie called his friend Paul Coverdell, who was at that time director of the Peace Corps, in hopes that someone from the Peace Corps in Honduras might travel with them around the Agalta Valley and discuss with them the potential of the ranch. They planned to visit the PrediSan mission in Catacamas as well as villages up in the mountains, and a local guide would make them feel more comfortable traveling the rural countryside.

Coverdell called the Honduras Peace Corps director, who asked the associate director for small business development to meet Archie and Joe at the airport. That man was not available, so Marco Fonseca filled in. As an associate director of the Peace Corps in Honduras, Marco had responsibility for agriculture and adult education. His primary duty was to identify potential work sites and write descriptions of projects for Peace Corps volunteers.

Joe and Archie liked Marco instantly. He had grown up near Tegucigalpa then came to the United States, where he earned degrees from Cornell University and the University of California

at Davis. Marco had been one of the first "exchange" Peace Corps volunteers—a Latin American serving in the United States—volunteering in Harlem from 1967–68, when, he reminded Joe and Archie, "the cities were burning, Martin Luther King Jr. was shot, Robert Kennedy was shot, and the Black Panther movement was growing." He married a Peace Corps volunteer from Boston and later worked for the Peace Corps in Puerto Rico before returning to his homeland.

Marco's father had grown up in Olancho, and although Marco had never seen Rancho el Paraiso, he knew much about the region of his father's childhood. He even knew a little of the history of Rancho el Paraiso, which had been owned by one of the most prosperous men in the region. Driving out to Olancho, Archie gave Marco his impressions of the ranch and his hopes for it, then asked for Marco's opinion.

Marco knew that Archie had already talked with many people about the ranch, and he hoped that his opinion would reinforce, not contradict, what Archie had heard. Marco believed the agriculture programs at the ranch needed to be developed quickly for two reasons. First, Honduran law allowed poor farmers, known as *campesinos*, to claim any land that was "not serving the social purpose" and put it into production. Crops were growing on fewer than one hundred of the ranch's sixteen hundred acres, leaving much of the property exposed to taking by campesinos.

Second, Marco believed the ranch could be much more than a place for North Americans to visit and do things for Hondurans. Agricultural training could help rural Hondurans see their potential. "If you can show a person his value, his potential, his worth," he told Archie and Joe, "then that person can do anything."

His belief was rooted in his family's experience. As a young man Marco's father had moved from Olancho to the north coast in search of good jobs offered by fruit companies. "Working for the fruit companies was like a gold rush," Marco said. "Subsistence farmers were attracted to monthly salaries. But they didn't realize all the other implications of moving to a place where they had to pay rent and other expenses. Until then, they had lived in their own house and farmed their own place. They did not know about a cash economy." Many of those young men went from one kind of poverty to another.

Marco also told Archie how education had transformed his family and could transform Honduras. "Education will give you the ability to see things and go anywhere," he said. "I have seen that in my parents. They never went to school, and my mother didn't learn to read and write. But she believed strongly that education was the only way for her children to move forward. She insisted we go to school."

The Fonsecas' commitment to education opened opportunities for them to serve in positions of responsibility in Honduras, and Marco's position with the Peace Corps had introduced him to people at all levels of government throughout the country—connections that would be valuable to the ranch. Joe and Archie began to believe that Marco was literally a godsend. They needed someone to run the ranch, and Marco sounded like the perfect candidate. Toward the end of the week, they asked Marco if he would consider taking the job. Marco asked for some time to consider, then he accepted the offer.

ARCHIE and Joe, through World Outreach, had essentially bought Rancho el Paraiso. They believed the ministry could grow to include other denominations and go far beyond summer programs for Church of Christ youth. Archie asked Jerry Eickhoff, a Methodist, to serve as chairman of the board of directors, and Jerry asked his friend and attorney, John Pratt, to serve on the board as well.

Meanwhile in Honduras, one of Marco's first tasks was to adequately register deeds and define the boundaries of Rancho el Paraiso at the courthouse in Juticalpa, the capital of Olancho. He also established Honduras Outreach as a legal entity in the country. Then he began creating training and farm support programs.

He introduced the farmers of the Agalta Valley to new and better varieties of cabbages, carrots, and beans. He showed

them how to grow tomatoes. He instructed farmers to use hybrid corn, but they had no seed to begin with and no money to buy it. In the valley, almost no one had cash for seed. Instead they held back some seed from the harvest each year to plant the next season.

Honduras Outreach could easily have given the farmers the seed they needed to switch to better varieties, but Marco advised against it. The farmers should buy their own seed. So he loaned them seed and fertilizer, to be repaid later, even if they had to borrow against the harvest.

"I knew from my father's time that farmers are honest people," he said. "They will go out of their way to pay their debts."

In addition to training farmers and loaning seed and fertilizer, Honduras Outreach bought several small grain-storage bins so farmers could store their corn at the ranch through the summer. Until then, all of the farmers had sold their grain at harvest time, when the price was low. By storing the harvest at the ranch, they would wait and sell it when the dry season came— when the price of corn was twice as high.

But even as Marco trained and supported farmers through the ranch, he learned from them. He explained to a farmer with apple trees that he needed to thin his apples. "It's as if you have five children or three children and the same amount of food," he said. "With fewer apples on each branch, they grow bigger and you can sell them for more."

"That's very good," the farmer said, "but here if I have three big apples, I have to sell them for ten limperas. But if I have ten smaller ones, I can sell them for two limperas each. A lot of people have two limperas. Not many have ten."

Marco realized that his technology was out of place in the economic world of rural Olancho. So instead he showed the farmer how to fertilize his trees adequately so that the larger numbers of apples wouldn't ruin the tree.

CHAPTER 6

DOERS OF THE WORD

So when He had washed their feet, taken His garments, and sat down again, He said to them, . . . "I have given you an example, that you should do as I have done to you."

John 13:12,15

THE REVEREND James Thompson of Decatur First United Methodist Church never imagined the impact on his life or the life of his church when he asked Jerry Eickhoff to speak on Laity Sunday in October 1989. He knew a little about Jerry's trips to Honduras earlier in the year, but did not anticipate they would serve as the inspiration for his message.

Jerry told the congregation about both trips—the good, the bad, and the ugly—contrasting those experiences with his financial difficulties created by the stock market crash. Several times during his message he became uncharacteristically emotional. Then he told the congregation he was going to do something to address the situation. He was going to gather a group of men and go back down to Honduras to build a milking barn. He didn't ask for help; he just explained what God had called him to do and prayed that God would touch the hearts of others who might step forward.

A week later Jerry suffered a kidney stone and was lying in bed at home when

Jim Thompson called. Jim had been touched by Jerry's message. He said Decatur First had been expressing mission support primarily through giving, and he was looking for ways to transform that into hands-on support of missions. He asked Jerry about the possibility of organizing a group from the church to go down for ten days and build that milking barn. Jerry thought that was a great idea, so Jim went to work recruiting.

Be doers of the word, and not hearers only.

James 1:22

DAN Pattillo is a doer. He retired in 1979 from the construction company he had cofounded with his brother and father—one of the largest in the Southeast—and for six years served as chairman of the board for the Metropolitan Atlanta Rapid Transit Authority. By 1989 he had retired from MARTA and felt as if he "wasn't contributing anything to anybody." When he heard Jerry's Laity Day message, he stepped up and offered to help with the milking barn, and soon he became the driving force behind the construction.

Dan recruited architect Joe Laseter, who designed the barn, and together they made a list of materials they would need:

lumber, concrete blocks, bags of cement, nails, galvanized steel for the roof, and so on. They sent the list, along with money to pay for everything, to Marco Fonseca, then rolled up their plans and were ready to go.

Meanwhile, Jim Thompson continued to recruit. More than anything, he needed laborers—people who could hammer nails, carry lumber, and mix concrete. Nearly everyone in the congregation met those qualifications.

The group also needed a nurse to accompany them in case of injuries or health problems, so they asked Fran Lewis, a registered nurse who is now trauma coordinator for Grady Memorial Hospital in Atlanta. At that time, Fran had been out of professional life for ten years as her children grew up. She had just finished graduate school and had not accepted a job. Although she did not feel called to go to Honduras, had never been out of the country, and wondered where the next bathroom would be once they flew south of Miami, she realized she was

at one of the few times in her life when she could make that kind of commitment.

But she was the only woman from Decatur who had agreed to go at that point, and she wouldn't go alone. So she called her friend Sue Church. Sue said no. She was scheduled to begin a major renovation of her home the week of the trip, so she couldn't go. Fran continued to prevail upon her, however, and Sue finally agreed to go. By the time the plane took off, three more women had joined the group.

Down in Honduras, Marco was gathering the materials Dan Pattillo had ordered. Trees were cut for lumber and floated down the river, then brought out and milled on site. A family that had a concrete block business at the riverside mixed sand, cement, and water, and packed forms with the concrete as quickly as they could.

By the day of departure in February 1990, the Decatur group had grown to thirty-two members. And at Rancho el Paraiso, Marco Fonseca had all of the materials waiting for them.

Every house is built by someone, but He who built all things is God.

Hebrews 3:4

MARCO met the Decatur group at baggage claim in La Ceiba and led them to a pair of El Negro buses. By the time they hit the dirt road, halfway to the ranch, night had fallen. The world around them was too black to see, and the noise from the bus and the bumpy dirt road made it too loud to talk, so one by one the exhausted group began to doze, awakening occasionally when the buses slowed down to ford a river.

When the buses finally arrived at the ranch and the engines stopped, silence immediately settled over the group. Headlights shone on the hacienda, where they would sleep. Marco led the group by flashlight to their quarters.

Sometime during the night rain began to fall. At first light on Saturday Dan Pattillo went out in the rain to the barn site,

a rectangular mound overlooking the hacienda, to inspect the construction tools and materials. He realized how unprepared they were for working in Honduras. He had shipped down a portable generator and the necessary power tools in advance. But the lumber, which had been cut and milled less than a week earlier, had not been given time to dry and was extremely heavy. Worse, the two-by-fours he had ordered were literally two inches by four inches. (In the United States, a two-by-four is 1½ by 3½ inches.) And the concrete blocks weren't anywhere near standard North American sizes. Joe Laseter spent much of the first day reconfiguring his drawings to fit the materials on hand.

After a breakfast of beans and rice cooked on the wood stove in the hacienda by Adelia, a local woman who took care of meals, the group went to work, joined by men from nearby villages whom Marco had hired to help with construction.

In the rain they dug footings for the concrete block columns. Then they hauled water up from the river to mix with cement and sand. They bailed the rainwater out of the footings they had dug and filled them with concrete. Sunday was not a day of rest. After worshiping in the church across the road from the ranch, they returned to their digging, mixing, bailing, and pouring. By Monday morning they were building roof trusses in the woodshed, where they could run the generator and electric saw without fear of electrocution.

AFTER CHURCH NEAR THE RANCH

We were working on the far wall of the barn, and we had rebar coming up out of concrete block. It was time for a two-by-six plate, but we needed holes drilled for the rebar. Somebody called, "Where's the drill? We gotta have the generator. Get the cord." Within twenty minutes we had the drill and the generator and the cord, and by that time one of our local helpers was just completing the last hole with an augur, and I'm sure he was thinking, "What are these people doing?"

Randy Mahaffey

ALL the time they were reminded why they were there. A group was taking a lunch break, and Joe Glenn sat down to eat a peanut-butter-and-jelly sandwich. Before long, a pair of hungry brown eyes was watching him from some distance. Joe motioned for the Honduran boy to come over, and when he did, Joe reached into his bag and pulled out another sandwich for him. The boy's eyes lit up as he took the sandwich with his dirty hands. Immediately the boy was surrounded by three other children, all eyeing the sandwich, and without hesitating, the boy broke his sandwich into four pieces and shared with the others. It wasn't the first time Joe had seen a Honduran be so quick to share. He had given toys to children who would play with them for a few minutes, then share them with another child.

After lunch he asked Marco why these children seemed so eager to share. "It's part of their culture," Marco said. "Families may have nothing for a month, and their neighbor who has something will share with them until the next month, when the family that had nothing will have enough to share. From their history they know they cannot do it alone."

WHILE the men were building, Fran and Sue took care of medical needs. "The main thing we did was pray that nothing would happen," Fran recalls. "The guys were doing major construction, building trusses and lifting them high into the air, walking the length of the building with them, then hammering them into place. We were so isolated, with no communication, that if someone had been hurt badly, we would have been in trouble. But our prayers worked."

There were two minor injuries. Dan Pattillo cut his hand on a barbed-wire fence early in the week. Fran treated it quickly and kept it dressed, so it never became infected. Another man threw out his back, and Sue's skills as a licensed physical therapist were vital to his recovery. When she began working on him, she didn't think he would be able to stand the bumpy trip back to La Ceiba at the end of the week. She worked on his back four times a day, and he slowly improved.

THE North Americans wanted to experience more of Honduras than just the barn raising, so on Monday morning Marco took Fran and Sue to the closest full-fledged town, San Esteban, so they could see the health clinic there.

The first thing Fran noticed when they drove into town was the dogs. They were everywhere. Sad, sorry-looking, hungry dogs. When Marco escorted Fran and Sue into the health clinic, a dog walked in with them. Another was already inside lying in the corner.

Fran and Sue were appalled, and they tried to tell the Hondurans that they needed to pen the animals up—and that

[Jesus said,]
"Freely you have received, freely give."
Matthew 10:8

[Jesus told his disciples,] "Whatever city you enter, and they receive you, eat such things as are set before you. And heal the sick there, and say to them, 'The kingdom of God has come near to you.'"

Luke 10:8–9

under no circumstances should dogs be in a health clinic, of all places. But neither of them spoke Spanish, and Marco was little help. The dogs stayed.

Marco left, but not before explaining to the nurses on staff, Miriam, Marta, and Susana, that Fran was also a nurse. They did not understand Sue's role; they had never seen or heard of a physical therapist.

The area just inside the front door of the clinic overflowed with people, some who had walked for miles to have infants treated for diarrhea or other illnesses. A woman brought her baby back to be examined by a nurse, who first needed to weigh the child. The only scale was the standard doctor's office type, and the base was covered with mud from the feet of every patient who had stepped onto it in recent days. Sue had to restrain herself from diving for the naked infant as the nurse took her from her mother and laid her on that muddy scale. She pointed to the child, then reached out, and the nurse handed her to Sue. Then Sue stood on the scale holding the infant and pointed to their combined weight. She handed the baby back to the nurse and pointed to her own weight. Stepping off, she took a pencil and paper and subtracted the two numbers, then pointed to the difference and to the baby. They got it . . . and Sue got it. Her whole purpose for being in the clinic that day might have been completed in that one small moment, a moment that could save the life of a child by preventing the spread of a parasite.

Next, an adult patient came in, and the nurse asked him to sit on the examination table, the kind that has a roll of white paper at one end so that each patient can sit on a sanitary surface. In this case it appeared that the paper was changed daily, not after each patient. As the nurse examined the patient, the day's first emergency staggered through the front door. A man so drunk he could barely walk had cut his head badly. Miriam decided to let him be Fran's first patient.

She led Fran, Sue, and the patient, supported by a friend, to a back room with a locker-room bench that sat about eighteen inches off the floor. A dog followed them in. Fran tried to shoo the dog out, but he wouldn't budge. The Honduran nurse instructed the man to lie on the bench, and the dog sniffed at the wound. Fran pushed his nose out of the way and stepped between the dog and her patient.

Fran looked around the room for sterile packages of suture but saw instead a large spool of black thread on a shelf. Then Miriam pulled off a couple of feet, cut it, and dropped it into a tray of liquid like none Fran had ever seen.

After a few seconds, Miriam took out the suture and gave it to Fran, along with a needle and needle holder for sewing the man up. The needle holder, which worked like pliers, was so old and worn that every time Fran pushed the needle against the

Because of Olancho's reputation for outlaws, the ranch initially had guards who openly carried AK-47 rifles day and night. Occasionally in the middle of the night, a guard would fire a round. "It was the only time the men's dorm was perfect silent for thirty seconds," Randy Mahaffey recalls. "No snoring, no talking, no nothing. We're all in there thinking there must be somebody out there. But I don't think there ever was. The guards just wanted us to think that. It was job security for themselves."

"Lord, give us this bread always."

John 6:34

man's skin, it turned in the gripper. There was no anesthesia, but the man had almost passed out from his drinking, so he didn't complain of any pain. Fran finished the job, and the patient's friend helped him stagger back out to the street.

AFTER they saw several more patients, the Honduran nurses suggested that it might be time for a break. Fran and Sue had brought packs of cheese crackers, expecting that to be their lunch for the day. Miriam, Suzanna, and Marta brought cold Cokes for everyone from the refrigerator. Sue and Fran shared their crackers, and the Honduran women shared their Cokes. "And as we sat at the table, each of us sharing what we had, there was unbelievable power in that moment—the power of Holy Communion," Sue says. "Fran and I looked at each other and knew in an instant that God had blessed our time in this place."

The afternoon brought no more emergencies, and near the end of the day the clinic staff began to clean up. One woman dipped a mop in a bucket of water near the back of the clinic and swished it back and forth across the floor all the way to the front door, through the dirt and blood of the day's activities, never dipping her mop in the water again.

Marco came to pick up Sue and Fran, who hugged their new friends and left, wondering who would ever be able to explain to these people the correlation between sanitation and health. Marco would have to. They ran out into the rain to the truck and simultaneously began spilling out their frustrations and their fears for the Honduran people, starting with the mop and working back to the dogs.

"It's ridiculous for all these animals to roam free," Fran said as she pointed to chickens and cows in muddy yards. Homes had no doors or windowpanes, so nothing stopped the animals from coming inside.

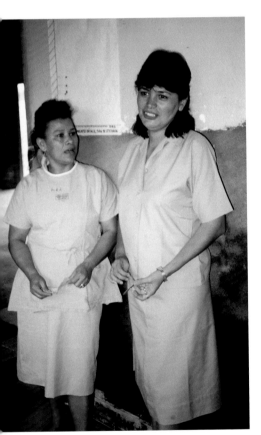

MARTA AND MIRIAM

"It can be no other way," Marco explained. "The people here do not feed their animals. They don't have that luxury. They can barely feed themselves, and the animals have to fend for themselves. If the people pen them up, the animals will starve."

The women realized they would have to seek common ground on this and many other issues. They had gone to Honduras planning to teach them the North American way, which they viewed as the *right* way, but they learned quickly that there are many ways.

Back at the ranch, construction continued in the rain. At night, over a supper of beans and rice cooked by Adelia on the wood stove, Fran and Sue described what they had seen in San Esteban. The women knew that they could not turn away from the people they had met. They had to do more. The entire group was beginning to realize that perhaps God had more in mind for them in Honduras than just a milking barn.

ADELIA

THE next day Sue and Fran returned to the little clinic, and they were finally able to communicate that Sue, as a physical therapist, helped people who had problems with their muscles and bones. The nurses insisted that she immediately go to see El Enfermo.

Five days before Christmas 1990, a Honduran boy, Arsenio, had fallen off a horse, hit his head, and fallen unconscious. The child was carried to his hut and placed on a pallet on the dirt floor, where he lay comatose for several days. There was little holiday celebration in the village of La Lima as family and friends gathered around the child to pray. Then before the new

Jim Thompson was Methodist, and I was Church of Christ, and we sat down together at the ranch and decided that if we were ever going to break down the barriers any place in the world, this is where it would happen, because there was very little religious influence there in the Agalta Valley. We also knew that the opportunity was bigger than any one group could do alone.

Honduras Outreach has allowed us to transcend denominational differences as we go down there. There are Presbyterians, Methodists, Church of Christ, Baptists, and other denominations, but we all profess to be servants of God who go with the purpose of sharing the good news of Jesus and helping the people of Honduras.

Joe Glenn

year arrived, the boy opened his eyes and, with help, sat up. But he was unable to move his arms or legs.

Arsenio became known as El Enfermo —"the Infirmed One." Day after day the family prayed that God would heal their son, but the child did not improve.

It was four o'clock, too late to get out to La Lima that afternoon, but the next morning Sue and Otoñel, one of the ranch employees, set out on horseback. There was, of course, no physical therapy equipment at the ranch—not even crutches. Sue begged some strips of inner tube, took a pocket full of candy, and picked up a stick that she could make into a cane if necessary. She and Otoñel rode east and forded the river, then passed through Dos Rios. All along the way, before they spoke to the people they met walking along the road, the locals would say, "Oh, you're going to see El Enfermo," and they would point the way to his house. Good news spreads quickly in rural Honduras.

They arrived in La Lima and were led to a hut among the village of huts. They stepped inside and found the boy with his parents. Two sawhorses with beans hanging on them to dry were the only furniture in the dark room. Sue relied on her best Spanish—six weeks in seventh grade—to explain who she was. They already knew, but Sue was relieved to find the Spanish words coming back to her. She knelt at the side of Arsenio and worked with him slowly, spending more than an hour to determine how stable he was. She feared that if she sat him up too quickly, he could have a massive stroke and die. As it turned out, the boy's muscles were fine. But because of the head injury, signals were not traveling from his brain to his muscles.

Sue asked the boy to move his arm, and he could not. Neither could he move his legs when she asked. Then she held a piece of candy close to him and asked if he would like it. He reached for it, and they all realized that the connections were there. He just couldn't think his way to a movement. He had to do it reflexively. He would have to learn again how to think signals to his muscles.

For the rest of the morning Sue used the inner tube pieces to lead the boy through resistive exercises. Then she and the boy's father got him over to the sawhorses, which Sue used as parallel bars. By afternoon Arsenio was standing and taking a few steps between the sawhorses. He and his family thought this was a miracle, and they were so excited that they wanted him to do more and harder exercises. But Sue was afraid he would overwork and have a stroke. She had him do less strenuous work, rewarding him with candy.

Riding back to the ranch at the end of the day, Sue thought about God's timely provision for Arsenio—a physical therapist at just the right time; the return of enough Spanish words for her to communicate with him; and sawhorses, the only furniture in the house but the perfect equipment for retraining the child.

The next day Arsenio was brought to the ranch, where Sue continued physical therapy, occupational therapy, and speech therapy for the rest of the week. By the end of the week, he was still the Infirmed One, but Dr. Steve Wilks traveled to Honduras a few weeks later and examined the boy. He determined that he would never fully recover, but Arsenio continued doing the exercises, and now he rides a bicycle and works for his father harvesting corn. He's no longer El Enfermo. They call him El Despacio—the Slow One.

ARSENIO

ON Thursday morning the men began hauling roof trusses from the woodshed to the barn site. The trusses, cut 30 percent thicker than standard and still green, weighed much more than normal

As a final gesture, the first group decided to leave the clothes and boots they had brought for the destitute Hondurans they had seen all week. Marco tried to gently persuade them to change their minds, but they wouldn't hear it. The Hondurans needed these things more than the North Americans did.

"Our thinking was, we have so much and they have so little," Joe Glenn recalls. "We wanted to give them what we had, so we would go down with our suitcases stuffed full and come back with them empty. But after awhile it was like bringing your children a gift from every business trip; pretty soon the only thing they are looking for is the gift."

trusses and required several men to lift them onto the framing. As they went up, several of the Honduran men working with them frowned and shook their heads. Someone from Decatur asked Marco what the problem was. "They say it's too steep," he said. "The tiles will slide off." But Joe Laseter had designed the barn with a metal roof, not tile, in typical American barn style.

All day Thursday and Friday the men built and placed trusses, and they wondered if they would finish. They would have to leave Saturday afternoon for La Ceiba so they could catch their Sunday morning flight home.

Before dawn on Saturday the rain had stopped, and Dan yelled, "Let's get to work! We're burning daylight!" They worked for two hours before coming in for breakfast. As the day wore on and it began to look like they might get the last trusses installed, huge clouds billowed up at the end of the valley. A thunderstorm would make it too dangerous to work on the roof, so they picked up the pace. Jim Thompson watched the cloud and prayed, "Lord, let us finish before it rains." The storm appeared to be moving directly toward them, then the clouds drifted toward the mountains. Finally the men lifted the last truss and nailed it into place. As they nailed up a palm branch to signify the topping out of the building, a rainbow appeared on the southeastern horizon. "It's the most beautiful rainbow I've ever seen," Jim said. "A sign of God's providential promise for this ranch."

The group hugged one another, prayed a prayer of thanksgiving, sang the Doxology, then put away their tools and cleaned up for the long trip to La Ceiba. As they left, many of them knew, as Jerry had known, that they would be back. The barn still needed a roof—Marco would hire local helpers to nail metal to the trusses— and a concrete floor. And if Rancho el Paraiso was to continue to offer North American youth opportunities for missions, they needed something more than the hacienda for their housing.

CHAPTER 7

NEXT STEPS

You did not choose Me, but I chose you and appointed you that you should go and bear fruit.

John 15:16

COMING HOME from Rancho el Paraiso feels like it must have felt to step out of the River Jordan after being dipped by the Baptizer himself. You want to take everybody you know back down to the river with you to share the experience.

Within a week of their return, several members of the Decatur group met to discuss next steps—and their next trip to Honduras. The vision was growing far beyond Jerry Eickhoff's plan to build a milking barn. They would work through Honduras Outreach to improve health services to people living near the ranch and make plans for an infrastructure that would support visiting groups.

For months Archie Crenshaw had been telling everybody he knew about Rancho el Paraiso. For some who heard, his telling became a call from God to get involved in the mission.

Kathy Edwards worked in development for Georgia State University and came to know Archie and Jerry through their fund-raising activities for the school. When Archie told Kathy

The reality of depending on God for your survival, for your very existence, and basic trust was something so evident in their lives and so lacking in my own.

Kathy Edwards

about Honduras Outreach, she was moved by his faith and passion. She believed that through him, God was calling her to a greater commitment. Prayer and more conversations with Archie and Jerry confirmed for her that Honduras Outreach needed someone with her skills and background in development. She was wrapping up a meeting over lunch with Archie when she told him she was leaving Georgia State.

"I'm sorry to hear that," Archie said. "Where are you going?"

"I want to come to work for you at Honduras Outreach," she said.

"You want to what? " Archie asked, "We'd love to hire you, but we don't have any employees in North America. We don't even have money in the budget for employees."

Kathy remained confident that Archie would be calling. A month later he did, and Kathy became the first paid North

American employee at Honduras Outreach—U.S. director. Her first major assignment was organizing a fact-finding trip in August 1991, six months after the barn raising, to meet with Honduran health officials. Sue Church and Fran Lewis would be going, and they recruited Dr. Hugh Spruell, a member of their Sunday school class. They set up meetings in Tegucigalpa and Olancho through contacts in the Peace Corps and the American government.

Before going down, Kathy, Sue, Hugh, and Fran spent several hours crafting their questions and translating them into Spanish. Honduran director Marco Fonseca met them at the Tegucigalpa airport and accompanied them to the meetings, translating the answers. They learned that in most areas of Honduras, government health clinics serve villages within a two-and-a-half-hour hour walking distance. In rural

Creating an Organizational Structure

At the time of incorporation, Archie Crenshaw and Joe Glenn, whose World Outreach Foundation continued to make mortgage payments, created a four-member board that included themselves, Jerry Eickhoff, and John Pratt, a lawyer and a participant in the first mission trip to the ranch.

Jerry and John's pastor, Jim Thompson, became the fifth board member, and his passion for the mission led him to become a volunteer chief executive officer. Jim's vision of a threefold mission—education, agriculture, and spiritual growth—remains the foundation of Honduras Outreach. He created nine committees and appointed leaders to oversee the various aspects of the ranch.

Jim was as passionate as anyone for Honduras Outreach, and many weeks he spent as much time on it as he did running the church. He used most of his vacation time to visit the ranch.

Olancho, however, many villages were too far from any clinic to receive health care. The government welcomed any help Honduras Outreach could offer. A coordinator in the Health Ministry told them of four villages where health clinics were needed desperately: El Pedrero, Las Manzanas, La Ensenada, and Pacura.

After two days of meetings in Tegucigalpa, Marco took the group out to the ranch and then to some of the villages where the government had proposed building health clinics. Along the way, he stopped in Las Delicias and introduced them to Dr. Maria Elena Solano, who had been sent by the Catholic

Church to provide health care. Dr. Solano's "office" was in a two-room mud hut with a dirt floor. She lived in the second room, which was separated from her office by a curtain, and she had a pet monkey that ran around the room.

Since none of the North Americans spoke Spanish and Dr. Solano spoke no English, Marco began translating for them. Then they discovered that Dr. Solano spoke fluent French, as did Hugh Spruell, and for the remainder of the meeting the two physicians discussed medical needs and opportunities in French. Dr. Solano agreed to work with Marco to gather information needed for the Honduras Outreach medical program.

THEN Marco took the group to Culuco, the village nearest to the ranch. Culuco was a mudhole—a literal cesspool. As the rain fell, garbage, which was scattered everywhere, became part of the stinking mud that pigs and children rolled in.

This village at the edge of Rancho el Paraiso was the poorest of the poor. The people had been brought there twenty years earlier as part of the nation's agrarian land reform. It was not their home. The government, in an effort to make better use of all the land in Honduras, relocated farmers to sparsely populated areas. Sometimes cattlemen assisted the army in relocating the poor away from their ranches by loading entire families onto trucks and taking them against their will to their new "homes." Some poor families were enticed with promises of new farmland and new houses. This is how the people of Culuco found themselves alone in the Agalta Valley, unable to sink their roots.

There was a cantina in Culuco run by a man known as Taco, who was also the unofficial village leader. The cantina had no

MARCO FONSECA

And she said, . . . "Even the little dogs eat the crumbs which fall from their masters' table."

Matthew 15:27

Sue and I were looking for miracles every day, and they abounded. We never worried if we were in a jam. We trusted in God for everything, and just when we needed it most, over the hill would ride the Royal Mounties in some form. It was awesome what He did.

Kathy Edwards

sign, but the men of the village knew where to find it. Those who could not afford a few lempiras for a drink from Taco made their own wine from the abundant coyol trees growing in the valley. They chopped down a coyol tree and dragged it home, then they chopped out part of the bud end of the tree. The little chamber they made quickly filled with sap, which fermented into wine. Because of the desperate economic conditions in Culuco and surrounding areas, many men relied on Taco or the coyol trees to ease their misery.

Marco introduced the small group of North Americans to the people of Culuco and explained that they wanted to help them, but first they needed to ask a few questions. They paired off, and Kathy Edwards found herself talking with an old cowboy who had a wide face with deep lines, several broken teeth, and a broad cowboy hat. Despite Marco's explanation, the man's questioning eyes told Kathy that he still did not understand what

she was doing. She had memorized her questions in Spanish and hoped he would talk slowly enough for her to understand his answers.

"How many times a day do your children get dairy products?" she asked.

The man's eyes softened and the corners of his mouth turned up a bit. Kathy saw respect and humor and compassion in his face, as if he were saying, *Poor child, you don't understand, do you?*

Then he said, "I can't think about how many times they get dairy products. I just have to think about whether they get food."

Only a wall separated him from those abandoned beings who lived gropingly in the dark outside the pale of the rest of the world; he was elbow to elbow with them. He was, in some sort, the last link of the human race which they touched. He heard them live, or rather, rattle in the death agony beside him, and he paid no heed to them! His thoughts were elsewhere, given up to dreams, to impossible radiances, to loves in the air, to follies; and all the while, human creatures, his brothers in Jesus Christ, his brothers in the people, were agonizing in vain beside him!

Victor Hugo
Les Miserables

The question presumed a situation far from the true condition. The starting point in Culuco was below anything Kathy had imagined. She had heard Jerry Eickhoff's story of the children and the milk, but she still was not prepared for what she saw and heard from this man.

Before arriving in Culuco, her imagination had been quick to run toward dreams and big ideas such as sophisticated health care programs for the people of Honduras. Her conversation with

In December 1990, Kathy Edwards went to Honduras alone to deliver presents for the ranch employees and their families. There was no group at the ranch, and Marco was in Tegucigalpa for a few days with his family. Kathy stayed alone in the hacienda, listening to bats flying in and out all night.

Apparently the staff had not expected her, because they had very little food on hand. By the second morning, she was tired and painfully hungry, and she lay in bed thinking, This is what these kids live with day in and day out. Do their stomachs hurt this badly, or do they get used to it?

She prepared herself for another breakfast of a tortilla and a few beans, and as she sat at the table, Adelia, the cook, brought over a plate with an egg on it. Kathy looked at it and instantly felt unworthy of the sacrifice made for her.

the cowboy brought her down to earth—and to the mud, which no one in Culuco washed from their hands or their food.

Reflecting later on the experience, Kathy said that visit to Culuco was divinely inspired and established the model for Honduras Outreach. "So many North Americans' efforts to help stumble out of the block because they try to go in and recreate a little North America," she said. "They tell people what they should do. It was God's wisdom, not ours, that led us to ask what they needed. Instead of trying to figure out what people need, we simply asked."

Back at the hacienda at the end of the day, Kathy, Sue, Fran, and Hugh had independently reached the same conclusion: anything they were worried about back home paled in comparison with depending on God every day for food and shelter. They also decided that Culuco, because of its horrible condition and its proximity to the ranch, should be a top priority.

THE group returned to the United States and reported its findings.
They had known all along that they would need much more
money than they could find in their own pockets, and the original
idea of a self-sufficient ranch had already proved unattainable.
Archie Crenshaw knew that PrediSan had received a grant from
the United States Agency for International Development (USAID),
and suggested that Honduras Outreach request a grant for the
health program. Justin Myrick, a Georgia Tech professor who had
written the PrediSan grant proposal, shared his paperwork, and
Kathy Edwards began putting together an aid request for
Honduras Outreach.

CHAPTER 8

BUILDING IN HONDURAS

"Which of you, intending to build a tower, does not sit down first and count the cost, whether he has enough to finish it."

Luke 14:28

DAN PATTILLO began making plans for a dormitory on the ranch. "We are never going to have big crowds of adults if the hacienda is the only place to stay," he told Jerry. "Fourteen of us are sleeping in a room the size of my office. If we expect more people to go, they have to have a place to take a shower and a kitchen that we can inspect."

His experience of building the barn had taught Dan that any construction project—and especially a large one—in Honduras would present problems he had not faced in the United States.

Joe Laseter designed a dormitory that would sleep thirty-two people and include four bathrooms, a kitchen, and a dining room, plus a long porch with rocking chairs facing a huge ceiba tree and the mountains beyond. Bill Floyd, whose construction company specializes in water and waste water systems, designed a septic system to serve the dorm and future growth of the ranch. They would need heavy equipment for a project of that magnitude, so Dan bought a Ford tractor and

shipped it down, and Bill donated a backhoe.

Shipping equipment and supplies to Honduras presented yet another challenge. Port officials in Honduras were routinely offered cash incentives by shippers to expedite the transfer from ship to shore. Or, stated more bluntly by Jerry Eickhoff, "We can pay a hundred dollars to get a guy at the port to turn his head so we can ship the generator to the ranch when we need it."

For many businesses, this was just a cost of operating in Central America. It was the way the world worked. The nucleus that would become the leadership of Honduras Outreach debated the pros and cons of following accepted protocol and decided not to compromise their principles. They would not pay what they considered bribes to dock workers. Their stance led to delays in shipments, but they believed consistent adherence would build credibility that HOI could rely on in an emergency.

They followed other governmental protocol closely, even when ignoring it might have allowed them to help more people. For example, physicians working through Honduras Outreach always register with the government before each trip in which they plan to see patients, and all shipments into the country are outlined and documented accurately and completely. "We have to respect the Honduran people, their laws, and their customs," Sue Church said.

Dan coordinated design, ordering of supplies, and shipment of material from the United States to Honduras. Care was taken

The lab person in the government health clinic had a stack of malaria slides she couldn't see because her microscope had no batteries for the light bulb. It was such a simple thing to give her all the batteries we had.

Sandy Patterson

to ship only those supplies
that could not be obtained in
Honduras. Wherever possible,
Dan and others wanted the
local economy to benefit from
the project.

The plumbing work stood
out as an example of Dan's
preparation. Few of the
Honduran workers had ever
seen plumbing, and the only
plumbing most of the Decatur
group had ever done was to
replace a washer or a faucet.
So Dan made the plumbing
"idiot-proof" for the North American volunteer workers before
he shipped it down. He bought all the necessary PVC pipes
and fixtures and had them delivered to a Pattillo warehouse.
Then he laid out all of the pipe, cut every piece to the proper
length, and put the entire system together without glue. He
color-coded and numbered the ends of every pipe with Magic
Markers so the "plumbers" could easily put the whole thing
back together again. Then, because he could not ship plywood into the country to build forms for pouring the concrete
septic tank (Honduras is a wood-producing country, so wood
cannot be imported legally), he designed packing crates to the
exact size of the forms he would need. When the crates were
unpacked, they became forms.

The group left Atlanta in February 1991, and over two
weeks the team built and installed the septic tank and laid
five drain fields, poured a concrete pad and installed a new
generator on top of it, and installed water heaters in the

Although he was primarily concerned with construction issues, Bill Floyd began to see changes in the Honduran people as well as in the Honduran landscape.

"I asked God last year to give me purpose in my life," Bill said when he returned in 1991, "and He did. When I went to Honduras last year, I felt He was part of what I was doing. But I realized over the course of the year that was not enough. I need to feel like I am helping the people of Honduras. This year I realized we are helping.

"You can make a commitment in an instant, but it takes time to earn someone else's trust. This year we began to see trust and hope in the eyes of the people—and not just the young people but also in the old people working in the fields."

dorm. They also completed some unfinished business from their 1990 trip by grading the floor of the dairy barn and pouring a concrete floor.

"But the most important thing we did," Doug McAfee reported upon their return, "was experience God's love. We had several people in our group who were in their sixties and seventies, and God gave all of us endurance to work twelve and fourteen hours a day. We mixed and poured twenty-one cubic yards of concrete for the septic tank and eight yards for the dairy barn floor. And there is no ready-mix concrete down there.

"Then my job was to dig the drain lines for the septic tanks, and I hadn't been on a backhoe in ten years."

When Doug climbed on the backhoe, he quickly realized that the levers were different from ones he had operated years earlier. The left-hand lever was on his right, and the right-hand lever was on his left. He paused and asked for God's help, and when he started up, it was as if he had been on that backhoe all his life.

Randy Mahaffey watched Doug dig the drain lines and said, "He could load uncrated eggs with that thing."

Dan never went to Honduras without Doug McAfee, who had been a building superintendent for Pattillo Construction for many years. "I won't go without him," Dan said. "He understands construction, and he understands my instructions."

Dan was surprised at how easily he communicated with the Honduran workers helping with construction. Even though he didn't know a word of Spanish (he put an O on the end of every word), he showed them the plans, pointed to the tool or hardware they needed, and described with motions what had to be done. And then they did it correctly—even the plumbing and wiring, which they had never seen before. Despite all his planning, after Dan left the country, things did not fall together exactly as designed. Some hot and cold water lines were reversed, for example, and when the slab was built eight feet too wide, the design had to be altered to fit.

ALL of the early construction trips to the ranch included a medical component. While others were building the dorm, Dr. Hugh Spruell conducted physical examinations for the ranch staff and their families. He set up a makeshift clinic in the hacienda, and by seven o'clock the next morning, dozens of people were lined up outside. Hugh did not speak Spanish yet, so Carolyn Fonseca, Marco's daughter, translated.

It didn't take long for Hugh to see the reality of death that the people of Honduras faced daily. The wife of a ranch employee brought her baby with a fever of 103. The child was otherwise healthy and reasonably well fed but had bronchitis and an ear infection.

Hugh gave the baby penicillin, but the next day the mother was back. The fever was down to 101, and she was still afraid. Hugh explained that it would take a little time. She had to be patient.

A mother back in America in the same circumstance, he thought, would call the pediatrician, get a prescription for amoxicillin, and pick it up at the pharmacy without a second

"I was naked and you clothed Me; I was sick and you visited Me."

Matthew 25:36

thought. But this woman instinctively knew that illness could kill her child.

Marco then told Hugh about several people he knew who lived nearby and were ill, so he and Hugh visited villages on horseback.

While Hugh was working near the ranch, the medical team of Dr. Steve Wilks, Sue Church, Fran Lewis, and Kathy Edwards visited the clinic in San Esteban. The clinic was led by a Honduran physician fresh out of medical school who had many more patients than he could keep up with. A long line of patients waited for immunizations, obstetrical examinations, and diagnoses of illnesses. The sicker patients moved to the front of the line.

Toward the end of the day, an extremely malnourished nine-month-old child was brought to the front for Steve to examine. The infant weighed only eight pounds. The baby's thirty-nine-year-old mother was pregnant, and she had a three-year-old child with the typical bulging abdomen of malnourishment tugging at her leg. The mother simply had nothing left to feed the infant. Steve asked about the woman's situation and learned that she had six more children at home with their alcoholic father, and she had lost two children in infancy.

In her poverty, the woman had been forced to decide which of her children to feed, the older, healthier ones or the infant. Steve was witnessing the result of her decision—a starving child. He managed to control his emotions while in the clinic, but it would be months before he could describe the scene without being overcome.

In another room Kathy was helping Fran with vaccinations when a little Honduran girl ran into the clinic yelling, *"Preñado! Preñado!"* Fran scrambled to reach her Spanish-English dictionary and looked up the word. "It means *pregnant*," Fran said. "I think we'd better help."

Steve, a radiologist, had said before coming to Honduras that he would do anything necessary, "But please don't ask me to deliver any babies." Fran and Kathy stepped into the examination room as Steve and the young Honduran physician gently prepared a pale, listless, teenage girl for delivery. As they timed her contractions—two minutes—the husband and grandmother explained to the clinic doctor that the mother had been in labor

Despite putting land into cultivation and doing necessary due diligence regarding deeds at the courthouse, campesinos moved onto the ranch property in 1991. Marco Fonseca went to the Agronomy Reform Institute and got an eviction notice to force them to leave.

Along with the order, the military gave Marco fifteen soldiers to come kick the campesinos out. The soldiers came with their guns to do their work, and Marco said, "No, you're not going to do that. I will take care of it."

"What are you going to do?" one of the soldiers asked.

"I'm going to the house of the leader," Marco said.

"You're going to what?"

"Listen," Marco said, "I have no intentions to get into a fight. If we start shooting, they will start shooting. If we fight, they will fight." With the help of the leader, Marco persuaded the campesinos to leave peacefully.

Not long after that someone living nearby started stealing cattle from the ranch. The thief would cut the best meat from the carcass and sell it, then leave the rest in the field to rot.

A group of neighbors came to the ranch and said they would take care of the thief; they would kill him. "Don't shoot somebody for stealing a cow," Marco said. So the people became their own guard and began looking after the ranch. They knew where the cows were, and they told the thieves not to mess with them. They could be as mean as they needed to be—without shooting—and soon the stealing stopped.

at home for eighteen hours. The midwife needed help, so they brought her to the clinic.

Night was falling quickly, and the clinic had no electricity. Kathy had brought her flashlight, so she shone it on the mother while a six-and-a-half-pound boy squeezed through that tiny cervix. The infant was blue and flaccid, and there was no spontaneous respiration. Steve suctioned and rubbed, but mostly prayed for the little boy, and after two or three minutes he began to breathe.

In the United States the baby would have spent a day in intensive care and the mother would have stayed in the hospital for a couple of days. In San Esteban, Steve sewed up the mother's episiotomy and sent her and her baby home with the husband and grandmother.

"I often pray that that baby's outcome was better than the infant we saw earlier," Steve said later. "But I don't know."

AT the ranch the next day, Dan, Hugh, and Joe Laseter took a break from their work to walk the site of the next major construction project, the medical clinic. In keeping with Central American architecture, they decided to build a U-shape structure with a courtyard, and Joe sketched a simple design. Dan, looking toward the hacienda at the line of patients waiting for Hugh to come back, wanted something larger. "This won't come close to meeting the need," he said. "But if we build it big enough to take care of the need, it'll cover half the ranch."

Knowing the facility couldn't be as big as they wanted, Dan, Hugh, and Joe made sure the facility was as efficient as possible. "The doctor needs to see as many people as possible in a day," Dan said. "When you see that line of people out there waiting to get in, you know that they have got to see a lot of people in a hurry."

CONSTRUCTION projects like the dorm and the health clinic were much too big for a church group to complete in a two-week trip. Dan knew that professional builders would be required to complete them.

After they came home, Jerry called his brother-in-law, Frank Tetterton, a residential developer, and suggested that he go down to Honduras with Bill Floyd and him to see the ranch.

Frank enjoyed fishing, so he asked Jerry if the fishing was any good down there.

"I don't fish," Jerry said, "but I've been told there's some tremendous bass fishing."

Frank packed his rods in their fancy boxes and got on the plane with Jerry and Bill. When they arrived at the ranch, Frank realized it wasn't a fishing trip at all. The first dorm was under construction, and Bill and Jerry discussed with him the water and sewer needs of the ranch as well as framing and

Compromise

In the United States, patients go to an examining room, and the nurse and doctor come in to see them. In Honduras patients move from room to room: first preclinic, then to another room to see the nurse, and finally to a third room to see the doctor. As they move, they infect every room along the way. We explained the problem with doing it their way, but they were adamant about not changing. So we settled on no dogs in the clinic.

Sue Church

other construction issues. Late in the afternoon of their last day, Frank said, "Jerry, I thought you said I was going fishing."

"Oh, that's right," Jerry said. He called over a couple of the ranch hands, who took Frank to a pond out on a dirt road. Frank pulled out his rods and reels and began casting. The other men unrolled string wrapped around a tin can, caught insects for bait, slung the hook into the water, and waited.

Twenty centuries earlier Jesus called his disciples by the lakeshore. In those few quiet minutes before the sun went down and they had to return to the ranch, Frank knew God had brought him here not to fish but to help. They got back into the truck, and he began formulating his response to God's call. He could bring down a crew of framers who could build more in a week than volunteer church groups could build in six months. When they arrived at to the ranch, Frank told Jerry that he was hooked.

"Follow Me, and I will make you fishers of men."
Matthew 4:19

A major component of the vision of Honduras Outreach from the beginning was the creation of health clinics—one at the ranch and four more in outlying villages. Frank Tetterton and his friend Millard Bowen, a home builder, brought a crew of framers, plumbers, and electricians to Honduras in 1992 to build the Dan and Anne Pattillo Clinic at the ranch.

The worst thing that can happen while a professional construction crew is on site in Honduras is to run out of building material. Because of a miscommunication, that's exactly what happened in the middle of building the clinic.

Mario Decarret, who had replaced Marco as ranch director, took Frank and a couple of men to

a sawmill in the mountains. The mill was in the middle of a job running a certain type of material and cuts, and Mario translated to Frank that they would not be able to get to their job for several days. "Show him some of these Benjamin Franklins," Frank said pulling a couple of $100 bills from his wallet, "and see if he'll change his mind." Within minutes the operator was reconfiguring the saw to cut the wood he needed. They loaded the truck so high, the tires looked as if they would burst coming down the mountain, but they had what they needed to finish the job.

As construction of the clinic neared completion, a group of adults from Decatur Presbyterian Church arrived to put on a tile roof. Nine women and five men signed up for the trip, and when they arrived, they were greeted by half-hidden snickers from the Honduran men on the ranch. How were a bunch of women—North American women at that—going to install a roof?

If the women weren't already determined to complete their task, they knew then that they would not leave Honduras until the last tile was laid. Like most North Americans, the women knew nothing about installing a clay tile roof, but they were quick learners. On Saturday morning they and the men set up a bucket brigade–type line to pass tiles up the ladder and across the roof. As the day wore on, the temperature on the ground climbed toward ninety. Nobody wanted to know the temperature on the roof.

Adelia, the cook, knew what they were up against, and at midmorning she came out of the kitchen with a twenty-gallon bucket balanced on her head. She was as big around as the bucket, and she walked carefully across the yard, hips swinging with the swishing of Hi-C filled to the rim.

The workers rested on Sunday and let their bodies recover from the heat and exertion. Then on Monday morning they went

I can do all things through Christ who strengthens me.
Philippians 4:13

at it early, before the heat took hold. By Tuesday afternoon they realized they would have to pick up the pace if they were going to finish. They had made believers out of the staff, who were doing what they could to help.

They finished the job on Thursday morning in time to celebrate, then clean up and get back on the bus to the airport, knowing that somehow God had given them the strength to accomplish a task greater than any they had imagined.

"If anyone serves Me, let him follow Me; and where I am, there My servant will be also. If anyone serves Me, him My Father will honor."

John 12:26

IN 1992 Honduras Outreach received the $500,000 USAID Maternal/Infant Survival Grant it had applied for a year earlier to provide health services in the Agalta Valley, and in building the staff, Jim Thompson made a critically important hiring decision.

José Mondragón likes to say he came to Rancho el Paraiso by accident. "I would not have known about it if I had not been in an automobile accident," he says.

At the hospital following his accident, José was referred to a medical clinic in Tegucigalpa. When he got to the city, however, he realized that he had not brought the referral paper with the clinic's address. José called a friend in the city to see if she knew of a doctor he could see. She did not, but they talked a little longer, and she told José that some North Americans were building a ranch out in Olancho and were interviewing for jobs.

THE North Americans had borrowed a room at the USAID office in Tegucigalpa to conduct interviews. José arrived at 11:30 and found that they had just taken a lunch break, so he waited.

"At 1:30, a man came in to where I was waiting and started talking," José recalls. "He spoke good Spanish, but his accent sounded a little French, like the Canadian priests. I had some bad experiences with Canadian priests, and I didn't like them much, so I didn't say much to this man—just yes or no when he asked me questions."

The man left the room, and several minutes later José was called in for an interview. The man from the waiting room introduced himself as Jim Thompson, executive director of Honduras Outreach.

What a nice opportunity I lost, José thought.

Despite José's reticence in the waiting room, Jim had many questions for him during the interview. José discussed his passion for education. When he finished sixth grade, José's father had said that was enough education. But José wanted to learn more, so he put himself through high school. Then he got a Central American Peace scholarship through USAID and went to Coffeeville, Kansas, for two years of college. He returned to Honduras with a background in accounting and a desire to be a high school teacher. He spoke fluent English, and Jim knew he would be an asset to the ranch.

José enjoyed the visit, but because he had no actual experience in accounting, he left the meeting expecting never to hear from Jim again. Jim, however, was determined to find a place for José, and he did. The USAID grant to the ranch included funds for a pharmacist in the health clinic, and José's background qualified him for the position.

JOSÉ

THE vice president of Honduras and the nation's minister of health scheduled an on-site visit to see the newly completed clinic at Rancho el Paraiso. Jim Thompson confirmed with Mario that his crew of Hondurans had completed the final details of clinic construction.

"No problem. No problem," Mario said.

Sue Church, Dr. Hugh Spruell, and Fran Lewis went down four days in advance to set up the medical equipment that had been shipped from the United States. When they arrived at the ranch, doors, window shutters, and a large section of tongue-and-groove ceiling had not been installed. They quickly became carpenters.

It was the first time Sue had met José, and they worked together, with Fran, installing a ceiling in the porch around the courtyard. Sue learned that José's mother had died only a few months earlier, while José was in the United States, and he had not learned of her passing until after the funeral. He was twenty-three years old, the same age as Sue's son, and they bonded as they worked together into the night. After a couple of days, construction was complete, and the equipment was installed and ready for their visitors.

José worked in the pharmacy for the next four months and also drove and worked with Dr. Maria Elena Solano to help select locations for satellite health clinics. Then a position opened up as special projects coordinator, which meant leading the groups of young people who came to the ranch in summer. Most of them were not much younger than José, and after living in the United States, he enjoyed introducing young North Americans to rural Honduras.

"When they come here they ask how people can live without a refrigerator or a television," he says. "After a week, though, they see that they can live without all of those things. They see

people smile without having all those beautiful things technology brings. They have a good time without those things."

CONSTRUCTION began on staff housing at Rancho el Paraiso with adult groups pouring foundations and building concrete block walls, and North American professionals led by Millard Bowen and Frank Tetterton doing the framing, plumbing, and electrical work. Millard hired Matt Moore after meeting him in Honduras—Matt was with the Decatur Presbyterian group working on the clinic—and Matt has since made more than two dozen trips to Honduras with his church and with Frank.

Since their first work on the clinic, Millard's crews have worked on most buildings at the ranch as well as kindergartens, medical clinics, and bridges built off-site. Millard pays their way and their salary for the week, and unlike the other groups who come to the ranch, these men are no church group. "Guys who do construction for a living are used to blowing and going," Frank says. "But sometimes we're working with a church group, and we

In 1992 Mirian Diaz became a secretary for Honduras Outreach. HOI rented an office in Juticalpa, one hundred twenty kilometers from the ranch, which had the nearest telephone line at that time. When forty telephone lines were run to San Esteban in 1997, the ranch bought a wireless phone with enough power to communicate with a base in town. Because of the limited capabilities of the phone lines, HOI could not send or receive faxes. So the Hotel Honduras in Juticalpa gave HOI a small space to keep a fax machine to send and receive messages.

have to develop a tolerance for people who can't climb on a roof and swing a twenty-foot two-by-ten."

Every night when they're in Honduras the crew gathers for a devotional. "I find that through devotions and a time of prayer, some burly, rough-and-tumble guys open up and start sharing," Frank says. "It's a very meaningful time for us, and it leads to one-on-one conversations between Christians and men who might be unchurched.

"But they are all deeply touched by the people of Honduras. Almost every time I go I have an opportunity to walk with people for the first time. They look in people's homes and they see what they don't have, and some of them are overwhelmed and touched by that. They want to give. They want to do something for their fellow man."

The crews do more than just build when they're in Honduras. They also teach. Millard will often add several Hondurans to the crew and teach them how to use a Skilsaw and a square. "We show them how we build things so they will stand the test of time," he says.

José Mondragón, named Honduran director in 1995, has learned North American ways as well. "When José first started," Frank says, "he was very young and didn't know much about construction. We would tell him, 'José, we want to be work at 6:15 in the morning, and we need this list of materials.' He'd say, 'No problem. No problem.' Then nothing would happen.

"But he quickly grew accustomed to the work regimen of North American construction workers—how they like to go from A to Z, and they want the right material at each step. Now he takes a pad, makes his own list, and makes things happen. Whatever they need, they get."

At the same time, the professional builders have learned how to work with people in Honduras. In the early days they

expected the job site there to be like their job sites back home. "For us, it was all about the finished product," Frank says. "The real message, though, is the journey—working with other people, mixing cultures, and finally seeing the finished product. It's a real blessing to drive to the ranch and see so many buildings and know you had something to do with that."

BUILDING AN AG PROGRAM

THE North Americans created a demonstration project at the ranch so that other farmers could see what worked well and

emulate it. Jim Thompson, who raised cattle in north Georgia, invited his veterinarian, Dr. Fred Ingle, to Honduras to lead the project.

Fred found the livestock in the Agalta Valley "in a terrible state. Like the people, they were underfed and suffering from malnutrition."

The farmers did not understand the correlation between salt and livestock health, and even if they had, they could not have afforded salt. A fifty-pound salt block, which cost $3.25 in the United States, costs $25 in San Esteban—nearly 10 percent of the annual income for most farmers.

Honduras Outreach began shipping salt blocks to the ranch and selling them for $3.25. Just through the provision of salt and minerals, cows that had been calving every two to three years began calving every year, doubling or tripling the ranchers' income.

Fred demonstrated other animal husbandry techniques to farmers who still were not convinced of the need to fence and feed their cattle.

"Their level of education is so small," Fred said. "They're like a dried sponge. Nobody has put any water on them."

In addition to training farmers to grow crops on a family scale, Honduras Outreach leadership hoped to grow enough crops on the ranch to feed visiting groups and also generate a profit. Several attempts turned out well, while others did not fare so well.

The ranch staff was not ready for the disease and insects that come with large-scale production. They planted one hundred acres of rice, and almost overnight millions of insects swarmed in from out of nowhere. The rice appeared to be moving, but it was actually grasshoppers on the rice. HOI was suffering the same problems as the farmers, but on a larger scale. When the cattle were bred with brown Swiss, the result was beautiful cattle that gave much more milk than the Brahmas. But they were susceptible to disease and ill suited to the Honduran climate, so that experiment was ended.

The agriculture program opened doors of trust between Hondurans and North Americans. Julio Rodriguez, who ran the agriculture program at the ranch, took Fred Ingle into the villages and introduced Fred as his true amigo. Then when Fred talked with them about livestock issues, they listened.

Julio later left the ranch and started his own business as veterinarian for the local ranchers. Every time Fred travels to Honduras, he shares a meal at Julio's home. The offerings differ from those he receives at the ranch—boiled cow's tongue, for example—but for Fred, a visit with Julio is like going home.

PARAISO'S GIVING TREE

ONE of the most magnificent sights on the ranch was a huge ceiba tree just beyond the hacienda. The ceiba tree is an important symbol in the Mayan faith, and it was easy to see why. It took ten people holding hands to reach all the way around the trunk, which looked like it had been growing there forever. Its limbs became home for thousands of orchids and colorful bromeliads, and higher up a family of owls built its nest.

Kathy Edwards sat and leaned against the trunk, feeling the security of the long limbs like arms wrapped around her. "It's like being under the protective wing of God," she said.

One of the men climbed high into the tree and tied a rope, then the women experienced the joy of little girls as the men pushed them higher and higher in the swing. When children came from nearby villages to see the North Americans, they took turns on the swing and played under the tree, protected by its canopy from the tropical midday sun.

One night in 1991, when the group from Decatur was building the dorm, a huge limb fell from the ceiba tree, barely missing the construction site. The Hondurans, never ones to waste anything, dragged it down to the river to replace the rotting limb that had served as their bridge from San Martín. The next year a larger section of the tree fell, and it too was used.

The tree that had represented so much to so many was obviously dying bit by bit. The limb that held the swing fell; the shade that had cooled the children disappeared; brightly colored orchids littered the ground; the owls flew away. Finally nothing remained but a termite-infested stump. Sue Church noted the spiritual irony of this symbol of the Mayan faith slowly succumbing to insects as the love of Christians grew up around it. She wanted to leave the stump to the bugs, but others feared that the termites would move from the stump to the dorm. They burned what was left of the tree. For two weeks the stump smoldered, and still it stood several feet tall with black chunks all around that looked like rocks. But at least the termites were dead.

Sue was teaching Bible school in Dos Rios when the local pastor, carrying a long log across his shoulder, stopped and listened at the window. Sue was having trouble with some Spanish words, so the pastor asked if he could help. He finished the story for the children, and after school he asked Sue if he could help with anything around the ranch.

"Can you build a cross for us?" Sue asked.

The pastor said he would use the log he had been carrying; it became the beam for the cross that stands where the ceiba tree once grew. As the cross went up, Sue began to have misgivings. Many Honduran Protestants reject all symbols, even the cross, as idols. Their churches are completely unadorned. Some Hondurans wondered if the cross was being placed as a memorial to the dead ceiba tree.

But for the Christian missionaries who come to Rancho el Paraiso, the cross stands a reminder of Christ's presence. It is the first thing visitors look for when they arrive at the ranch, and almost every morning a group will stand at its foot for devotional time and to experience Christ in their midst.

CHAPTER 9

HOSPITALITY

"I have called you friends."

John 15:15

RANCHO EL PARAISO was wide open during the early building years. Visitors from nearby villages and all the children living in the orphanage came to play, sell handmade items, or ask for candy. The ranch was a place of mutual hospitality; Hondurans welcomed North Americans to their country, and the visitors welcomed the Hondurans to their home away from home.

One afternoon Santos Lopez, a little boy from San Martín, came running to the ranch. *"¡Venga conmigo!"* he cried. *"¡Se muere mi abuelo!"* Santos's grandfather was dying, and he wanted people from the ranch to come.

The entire youth group visiting the ranch along with their adult leaders followed Santos back to his hut in San Martín, which by then was surrounded by everyone from the village. Santos led the North American children inside, where they found the old man lying on his bed surrounded by candles and his family. The children bowed their heads as the family prayed in Spanish. Then

one of the adults communicated to the North Americans that
they would like for someone to read the Twenty-third Psalm. One
of the youth, who had grabbed a Bible before leaving the ranch,
read in English. More prayers were spoken, and when they filed
out of the hut, the little children of San Martín ran over. When
the first North American teenager put a Honduran child on his
shoulders, all of the Honduran children wanted a ride. The
group laughed and skipped back to the ranch, where they
played soccer until the North American young people were worn
out, and the Honduran children walked back to San Martín.

The next morning Santos, somber again, walked back to the
ranch and approached a group rocking on the dorm porch. He
asked if they could help him build a pine box. His grandfather
had died in the night.

Rather than build a casket, Matt Moore and two men from
the ranch drove a pickup truck out to Gualaco, where a man
built caskets, and bought one for Santos's grandfather. They

loaded the casket onto the truck and headed back to the ranch. About halfway home, another truck sped up from behind and attempted to pass on the bumpy road. The driver of the other truck yelled out his window, *"¡Amigo, amigo!"* and signaled for them to stop. They did, and the other driver pointed to the back of their pickup. The casket was gone. Their new friend said it had fallen out about a mile back, so they went back to pick up the pieces. Fortunately, the damage was minor. They loaded it back onto the truck and drove back to the ranch, where they patched it up before driving over to San Martín.

Señor Lopez was placed in the casket, and that night Matt and the youth group helped keep an all-night vigil with Santos and his family. Allison Per-Lee, the youth group's leader, says of her experiences, "Our kids came back from Honduras talking about how spiritual the Hondurans are. They saw that the Hondurans have no material things, and they realized how distracted we are by money and prestige.

"Children are very spiritual. The deepest desire that both children and adults have is for God. At the same time, children are in the process of understanding their identity. They want to get in touch with who they are as a child of God created in the image of God. Honduras helps them do that better than any mission I've been a part of.

"Our kids come home longing for the kind of simple spirituality they have seen, and they realize that our culture is not the best place to develop that relationship with God. When they are in Honduras, all of the pressure for money and success is stripped away, and they can recognize that desire for God. They can get in touch with it more down there."

DAN Pattillo, despite strong requests to the contrary from HOI, had brought all kinds of toys—balls and trucks and bulldozers—

As we were leaving the restaurant in Juticalpa, I packed up some left-overs to take. We were getting back on the bus, and a kid crawled out of a Dumpster. He was carrying a wash-basin, and he went to the empty tables to gather scraps. I told Bob Hope that I would be back. I'll come back every year until I run out of money.

Andy Sewell

and when word spread through the valley, dozens of kids lined up outside the dorm to play with them.

"I knew I wasn't supposed to do it," Dan recalls, "and I admit I took some things they didn't need. But if you could see the faces of those children . . ."

Santos Guzman spent much of his time at the ranch visiting the North Americans and hoping for a candy treat. When he heard that one of the gringos had brought a whole sack full of toys, he raced over to see what was up.

The line was more than twenty children long when Santos arrived. He waited patiently, and when he finally moved to the front of the line, he was enchanted by a big yellow remote-control dump truck. He made it go forward and back, and he pushed a button to make it dump its load. When Dan's group returned to Tegucigalpa to catch the plane home at the end of their trip, he left the toys behind, and he made sure that Santos got that dump truck and all the batteries he had taken. He had heard that Santos had several brothers and sisters, but there was sorrow in their family. Santos had a brother who was born with Down syndrome, and his parents didn't know what to do with him. He didn't respond to them as he grew, and hardly moved from his lying position. After several months they lost hope and decided to leave him in the corner of their hut to die. Dan thought maybe that truck could bring joy to the family.

At dinner in Tegucigalpa, Dan wondered aloud if he had done the right thing by giving Santos the truck. Maybe he shouldn't have given away so many toys and encouraged those poor Hondurans to wish for things they could never attain.

Dan's doubts followed him home. Then, a week or so later, the rest of the story was relayed from the staff in Honduras back to Atlanta.

Santos took his dump truck back to his hut in San Martín and started pushing buttons. The truck went forward and back, beep-beeping while in reverse, and dumped its load on the dirt floor. Santos's little brother, the one with Down syndrome, watched from the corner, then pushed himself up and tried to move toward the truck. He struggled to get his knees up under him and finally began to crawl. Santos yelled, and his mother came running. She stood at the door weeping as her child crawled toward that Tonka truck. Then she scooped the boy up and held him close, smothering him in kisses. Filled with hope, the family began taking care of their child, who, though limited by his disability, grew in his family's love.

THE first of four outlying clinics built with support from Honduras Outreach was at El Pedrero, a village so remote that North American building crews could not work there. So HOI provided materials and oversaw construction, then hired a nurse to work in the clinic when it was completed.

No one forgets his or her first trip to El Pedrero.

Dr. Maria Elena Solana, the ranch physician, asked Dr. Lee Woodall, who was visiting with his church, if he would like to see the health clinic out there. That sounded interesting, so they took the ranch Jeep and drove east for two hours until they reached the Rio Sico Grande. Maria Elena directed Lee, who was driving, to turn off the main dirt road onto two parallel ruts that led into the woods. Lee drove through the forest until the ruts stopped at a trailhead. He parked the Jeep, and he and

The first time Dr. Steve Wilks made the trip to El Pedrero down the trail and across the river in the dugout canoe, he felt he was stepping into the pages of National Geographic. When he arrived in the village, he heard a familiar clacking sound. Investigating, he walked over to a hut, where he was offered a Coca-Cola and invited to play pool on a slate Brunswick pool table, and he wondered how in the world it got back there.

Maria Elena walked from there down to the river, about a forty-five-minute hike, where they found a dugout canoe. They crossed the river in the canoe, then hiked farther until they came to a clearing that was El Pedrero.

People were working on their fires and doing their chores in and around their mud huts, and a woman was killing a chicken on a stump and then cleaning it.

Maria Elena and Lee spent the day in the clinic with the nurse treating typical illnesses, colds, and diarrhea. Toward the end of the day, as the breeze blew smoke and the smell of roasting chicken through the clinic, a cowboy rode in on a horse. The man was filthy and exhausted and had apparently ridden for hours to reach El Pedrero for treatment.

He had a large ulcer on his leg, cutaneous leishmaniasis, caused by a parasite carried by sandflies. Unusual even in

Honduras, the ulcer had become prevalent around El Pedrero.
Maria Elena injected medicine into his wound and sent the man
on his way.

By that time it was late in the day. Lee and Maria Elena
knew they had to leave soon; it was the rainy season, and they
wanted to get back to the ranch before nightfall.

But when they stepped out of the clinic, there stood a
woman with an invitation to dinner. It was the woman who had
killed the chicken. Lee understood immediately the sacrifice this
woman was making. In a place where the diet consisted almost
exclusively of rice, corn, and beans, chicken was a luxury
reserved for only the most important occasions. Despite warnings
against eating food prepared in the villages, he and Maria Elena
stayed and enjoyed their meal and the woman's hospitality before
hiking back to the dugout canoe.

*"She out of her poverty put in all
that she had, her whole livelihood."*

Mark 12:44

EYE-CARE MINISTRY

At the last minute while packing for a trip to Honduras, Dr. Alan Kozarsky decided to bring several artificial eyes—a couple of dark ones and one or two light-colored ones. The last day we were in the country, a young Honduran man came in to be treated. In addition to his current condition, he had been in an accident years earlier that had terribly damaged one eye. He had lost the vision in that eye, and the cornea had scarred over so that it looked awful. In Honduras, young people with crossed eyes or other visible ocular problems carry a social stigma. That's the way it was with this man, who was in his forties and still single. Alan asked if he would like to try a prosthetic eye, and the man was hesitant. But Alan showed him how simple it was to put on, so he fitted it, and the man looked at himself in the mirror. His face filled with a huge grin. If I had passed him on the street, I couldn't have told the difference in his eyes. Alan had changed his life in that moment.

Dr. Steve Wilks

DR. Steve Wilks, a radiologist, was doing general medical screening in Pacura in 1992 when a young mother brought her infant daughter, Diana, into the examination room. The baby appeared to be blind, and after examining her, Steve confirmed for the mother what he assumed she already knew.

"I'm afraid Diana will probably never see," he said.

The shock on the mother's face told Steve that she had not suspected that her baby was blind, and he was instantly overcome with guilt for having appeared so callous. He determined to do everything possible to give Diana her sight again.

When Steve returned to Atlanta, he called Dr. Alan Kozarsky, one of the leading cornea specialists in the country. Alan and Steve both practiced at Piedmont Hospital in Atlanta and knew each other casually, and when Steve explained that a Honduran baby might need eye surgery, Alan agreed to examine her. Steve arranged transportation for Diana and her mother, Rosemary, to Atlanta.

Alan did all he could for Diana, but she remained blind. Later he casually remarked to Steve, "Maybe I ought to make a house call someday."

"As a matter of fact," Steve said, "they need an ophthalmologist to take care of people with cataracts around the ranch."

Alan quickly began backpedaling. He hadn't expected to be taken literally. "Steve, you couldn't ask me at a worse time in my life, as far as being busy in other issues, to go down there."

"Alan," Steve said, "you'll find that this is the best time in your life to go down there."

In early 1993 Alan and Steve went to Juticalpa to see cataract patients. "Against everybody's advice that you need months and months of planning and truckloads of stuff to do this, just an ophthalmologist and a radiologist and a little help from the local folks was all we needed to help some people," Alan recalls.

One of the patients, when her bandages were removed, said, "I have seen God!" Others cried when they saw their grandchildren for the first time. Alan knew he would be back.

Alan and Steve were in Tegucigalpa preparing to return home when Alan had a sinking feeling that he was abandoning his patients without having alerted a local ophthalmologist. Someone in Honduras needed to know what he had been doing. They asked around and found the medical school in Tegucigalpa, then they took a cab to the school and were directed to the eye clinic. Walking into the clinic, they met a young doctor in a long white coat who spoke a fair amount of English. "If any people in Juticalpa have postoperative eye problems," Alan told Dr. Carlos González, "it's our doing, and I hope you will help take care of them."

Dr. González said he would help under one condition: "If you ever come back, I want to go with you." He was an ophthalmologist and a trained cornea specialist who had read several of Alan's articles in medical journals. "He became my true brother in Honduras," Alan says.

Meeting Carlos quickly changed the developing model of care for eye patients through Honduras Outreach. "We found that Honduras has a significant number of well-trained, motivated ophthalmologists," Alan says. "They can tell us where we should go, what we should do, and work with us."

Alan's primary role since then has been to demonstrate efficiencies developed in the United States. "Working out of the Lion's Eye Hospital in San Pedro Sulo with one American ophthalmologist and one Honduran ophthalmologist, we can see twenty-five to thirty patients a day," he says. "This is a

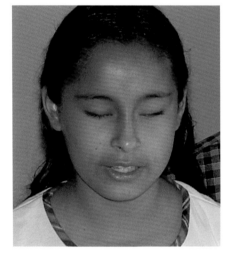

DIANA

huge leap from the four or five we saw our first day."

They ran into problems, however, because Honduras did not have an eye bank. So in 1996 Carlos spent over a month in Atlanta with Alan. He studied the eye bank there so he could create a similar one in Honduras. He also worked with Alan to learn vision correction surgery. He returned to Honduras with two goals: to open an eye bank and to determine whether they could offer refractive surgery. The answer to both was yes, and in 2002 the Alan Kozarsky Refractive Surgery Center, so named to honor Alan for his commitment to Honduras, opened in Tegucigalpa.

"It was your influence," Carlos said, "that led to this."

But Alan says Honduras has had a greater impact on him. "It's easy to forget that I got into this profession to help people. The Honduras Outreach experience is a refresher course every time I go. I am reminded that we North Americans are rich beyond measure. The disposables we use and throw away with every patient, they can't afford as permanent objects. Each trip gives me perspective I couldn't find any other way."

He credits Steve Wilks with opening his eyes to the need. "Steve is a world-class neuroradiologist who goes down there totally without ego," he says. "In Honduras he will be a nurse, he will be a technician, he will wash instruments, he will facilitate and do anything it takes to make things happen, even though it has nothing to do with his own extreme expertise. That is an example for me."

THE village of Tezapa was dying. Its children were malnourished and dehydrated from constant diarrhea. Their parents, many of them also sick, watched helplessly, or simply lay on the dirt in their mud huts awaiting death. Tezapa was five miles away from the nearest water source, a dirty river. With water so precious, the people didn't "waste" it by washing vegetables or hands. They had never been taught to boil water, so in addition to malnutrition, parasites plagued the village.

They were too far up in the mountains to be served by a government health clinic, but they managed to get word out that they were dying. The Honduran Ministry of Health had asked Honduras Outreach to assess the situation.

In a few days a group from Decatur Presbyterian Church would be arriving at the ranch. Dr. Maria Elena Solano knew that a doctor would be in that group, so she delayed her trip to Tezapa. She thought she might need the help of another professional.

When the North Americans arrived, Maria Elena loaded a van with medical supplies, food, milk, vitamins, and vegetable seeds for the village. Then she and the ranch nurse, along with medical resident Sissel Topple, Matt Moore, Sue Church, and a driver headed out.

Tezapa was almost in Colón, the next state to the north, and could not be reached by vehicle. Instead, the group from the ranch had to park at the top of a mountain, then walk down into the valley and back up the next mountain to the village carrying supplies. Every tree on both mountains had been cut down and sent to the lumber mill, so by the time they reached Tezapa in the hot sun, they were drenched with sweat.

The daughter of missionary physicians, Sissel Topple had grown up near a Korean leprosy colony. She knew the face of misery. But even she was unprepared for what she saw, and her North American companions wondered, in the midst of so many sick and malnourished children, if they would be able to control their emotions enough to gather the information needed by the Ministry of Health.

There was no way to treat everyone who needed attention, so Maria Elena and Sissel decided to treat the youngest first,

The mural behind the serving line in the original dining room was created by staff members who each painted something about the ranch that was important to them. Blas painted vegetables. Chito painted cattle. Tino, who was single at the time, painted his bicycle. Jesus painted bananas. José painted his family.

When the staff asked Sue Church what she would paint, she said, "There aren't enough spots for all the things here that I love." But they pressed her for an answer, and she said, "I would draw a church with a rainbow and a heart."

So the staff painted that for her with embellishments and added her favorite Bible verse, "Be still, and know that I am God" (Psalm 46:10).

The LORD preserves the simple;
I was brought low, and He saved me.
You have delivered my soul from death,
My eyes from tears,
And my feet from falling.
I will walk before the LORD.
In the land of the living.

Psalm 116:6, 8–9

seeing only those children who were no more than five years old. When Maria Elena explained their decision to the village, one mother cried out in anguish, and her husband came forward carrying a tiny boy. "He is six years old," the mother cried, "but he is dying."

How could he be six years old? the North Americans wondered. He was barely bigger than a newborn. "*Su nombre es Joel,*" the mother said.

Joel's legs were swollen from a lack of protein, and he was unresponsive. The nurse turned to Sissel and whispered, "This child is going to die."

"Really?" Sissel asked.

"Yes, this child is going to die."

"Then we need to get him back to the ranch."

The nurse did not believe the parents would allow Joel to be taken away, but they finally relented, as long as the father could go as well. It was agreed, and Joel's father, Pedro, carried him down the mountain and up to the van, where he sat on the spare tire in the back with Joel in his lap, bouncing for hours to the ranch.

Joel weighed fourteen pounds. To survive, he would require almost constant attention. Sissel treated him with oral rehydration fluid, gave him medications for pneumonia and antibiotics for various infections, and treated him for lice. (She got lice herself from Joel.)

Sissel checked on Joel every day, and was pleased when he could turn his head and surprised the next day when he sat up in bed. Two days later, however, when she looked in on Joel, his bed was empty. *Oh no*, she thought, *have they given up and gone home? Or has Joel died?* Then she looked down and Joel was standing at the door, barely up to her knees. He was medically

stable when she returned to the States at the end of the week
and another medical team arrived.

Joel required continued close attention, but the medical team
could not devote the time he needed; they had other villages to
visit. One member of the group, however, did not have health
care training, hated the sight of blood, and had said as she left
Atlanta for Honduras, "I have no idea why I'm coming." Now
Susan Hope had her answer. She was the one who had time to
take care of Joel. Susan fed him tiny portions of a milky porridge;
his stomach was so small, he couldn't eat more. He continued to
gain strength, and after a few more days he went to the kitchen,
where the cooks gave him food—which he promptly threw up.
That didn't stop him from going back, and the cooks could not
bear to turn him away empty-handed, so Maria Elena put a lock
on the kitchen door.

While Joel was growing stronger, his father, Pedro, worked
with the ranch staff, learning to grow food and tend animals. He
had a brief course in the care of goats and fencing gardens.

The medical team, plus Susan Hope, returned to Tezapa
with a healthy Joel, along with seeds, fertilizer, goats, and
other things. Their first stop was his house for a tearful
reunion with Joel's mother. Maria Elena told her how Susan
Hope had fed her son slowly and patiently, and how Joel had
gradually gained strength. The mother looked lovingly at Susan
as Maria Elena translated Susan's last name to Spanish,
Esperanza. The mother's tears flowed again.

Pedro told his village about the ranch and the things he had
learned. He became a village leader, teaching others how to
raise vegetables, and when the Heifer Project provided a pregnant goat for every family in Tezapa, he taught them how to
manage their herd for milk and meat.

JOEL

Behind the kindergarten that sits across the road from Rancho el Paraiso, mothers are learning better ways to ensure their children survive the early years. In a region where infant mortality is high, hunger remains a dreaded enemy.

Every week several cases of acute malnutrition arise in nearby villages. Like any other news in the Agalta Valley, information about the ranch nutrition center travels by word of mouth. Mothers bring their starving children to the clinic for treatment, but instead of medicine, they are given a one- or two-week stay at the nutrition center.

"It's part of the medical program," José explains, "but the children aren't sick. They're just hungry. Their families cannot afford food, or sometimes they don't know what's good for kids."

While living at the nutrition center, mothers have access to a kitchen, and the ranch provides food and small bedrooms. As the children grow stronger physically, their mothers learn how to prepare a nutritious, balanced diet for their families, which have little or no income.

A few days before a Presbyterian youth group arrived in Honduras, residents of San Martín had gotten mad at farmers living below the ranch and had cut off their water supply. Unfortunately water to the ranch was cut off as well. The youth had to bring water from the river every day to be boiled for drinking, and they had to wear their bathing suits down at the river every afternoon to bathe after working in the villages.

One afternoon when they were splashing in the water, the children of San Martín came to play. "Let's wash their hair," one of the North American girls said. So they passed the shampoo around and began washing the Honduran children's hair. Then Allison Per-Lee, their leader, waded past one of them, and she saw that the little girl's head was full of lice.

"You have to stop," she told her kids. "You're all going to get lice."

"We don't care," one of the girls said. "We love these children, and we want to finish."

So instead of making them stop, Allison sent one of the boys up to the ranch to tell Dr. Mary Elena Solano what was happening and to see if she had anything to keep her youth from getting lice. The boy came back with a big brown bottle with a label written in Spanish and a skull and crossbones at the bottom. All of the children washed their hair with it and came up from the river lice free—and with a new understanding of what it means to serve God's children as Christ would serve them.

FOUR North Americans stayed at the ranch for extended periods in the spring and summer of 1993, a time that made a lasting impact on them and on the ranch.

The ranch manager resigned a few weeks before the summer season, so Allison Per-Lee, who had left church youth ministry to serve as U.S. director of Honduras Outreach, went down to

Low-Tech Is High-Tech in Honduras

Hospitals and physicians sometimes donate outdated medical equipment to the ranch. For example, Dr. Phil Potter donated an ultrasound machine to the health clinic at the ranch. Initially Dr. German Jiminez used ultrasound almost exclusively for obstetrical examinations. Then Dr. Potter showed him how ultrasound can become a powerful diagnostic tool.

"A general surgeon was visiting the ranch and working in the health clinic examining and treating patients," Dr. Steve Wilks recalls, "when a ten-year-old girl came in with a high fever. Based on her symptoms, the doctor decided to investigate further with the ultrasound machine, and he found a large pocket of pus on the left lobe of her liver."

Without ultrasound the infection might have gone undiscovered, and even if it had been diagnosed, the only way to remove it would have been surgery. "That would have meant a trip to Juticalpa," Steve says, "and she might not have made it. With the ultrasound, we were able to localize the problem, and we got sixty cc's of pus—twelve tablespoons of 'pea soup.'

"The next day we were leaving for the airport, and the girl was sitting up outside with her mother with no fever.

"When you have nothing, little things and used equipment that might be outdated in the States can do a world of good."

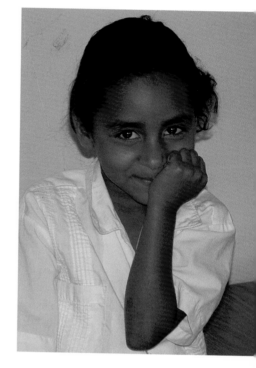

oversee ranch operations for the summer. Matt Moore, a retired army general, spent six weeks coordinating construction projects. Chris Hudson, a seminary student from Texas, directed four college students who were group coordinators. And Dr. Sissel Topple, in her second year of residency, spent two months in the spring working with Dr. Maria Elena Solano.

Rancho el Paraiso was isolated but not lonely. The only communication with the United States was through a ham radio, and every night Allison tried to call home—sometimes successfully, sometimes not. A couple in Texas who supported

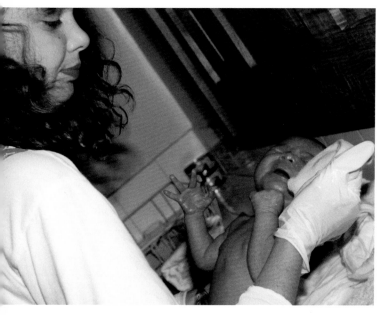

NEW LIFE IN PARAISO

missionaries around the world patched her by telephone to her husband, Phil. And at noon each day she called Jerry Eickhoff—again, with limited success—with news from the ranch.

Matt—known as *Mateo* by the Hondurans—worked with Millard Bowen and Frank Tetterton's crews to finish the two duplexes that summer for staff housing before the youth groups began arriving. Antonio and Daniel Lopez spent so much time working with the crews, they could have qualified as second-class carpenters in the U.S. Daniel was Santos's father, and it was his father for whom Mateo had brought a casket.

The first child born in the clinic came that summer, and Allison was there experiencing the power of new life. With youth groups coming every two weeks, she always felt connected to home. And when Phil came down for a week, the staff decorated a honeymoon suite in the hacienda. The staff was always looking out for her, and that's what she remembers most fondly—the relationships more than the accomplishments. "It sounds sentimental," she says, "but that's what continues to take me there."

Chris Hudson had grown up in a multicultural community long before the term was in vogue. His mother taught at an international boarding school thirty-five miles southwest of Corpus Christi, Texas, and the family lived on campus. He made friends from all over the world, as evidenced by the basketball team's starting five his junior year. He liked to tell people, "We had a kid from Japan, a Brazilian of Chinese descent, an Aztec Indian from southern Mexico, a Chicano Mexican, and a white kid, me." Chris learned the meaning of unity through that experience.

José Mondragón had started working at the ranch several months before Chris became summer youth director, and the two became fast friends. Chris loved Honduras and Rancho el Paraiso so much that when he and Monica were married the following year, he convinced her to honeymoon in Honduras, including three nights in the hacienda honeymoon suite.

WAITING AT THE PATTILLO CLINIC

FROM the looks of the wound, it must have been at least a week, perhaps two, since a seven-year-old boy had sliced two toes off the outside of his right foot while cutting grass with a machete. His family had treated him by packing the wound in coffee grounds, and when they finally brought him to Rancho el Paraiso in the hope of receiving better treatment, the foot was quickly dying.

Sissel Topple believed they could save the foot without surgery, but she couldn't be sure. Her father, a missionary and orthopedic surgeon, happened to be in the United States for a conference. If Sissel could confer with him, she would feel better about her decision.

Using the ham radio, she contacted a couple in the States who helped track down her father. They were patched in by telephone, and Sissel's father confirmed that wet-to-dry dressing would allow her to take away the dead tissue without surgery. The treatment was horribly painful, but with antibiotics the infection was eliminated. Chris Hudson made a crutch for the boy, and after several days the family was able to take their son home.

CHAPTER 10

BUILDING BRIDGES

We are God's fellow workers; you are God's field, you are God's building. According to the grace of God which was given to me, as a wise master builder I have laid the foundation, and another builds on it. But let each one take heed how he builds it. For no other foundation can anyone lay than that which is laid, which is Jesus Christ.

1 Corinthians 3:9–11

AFTER FIVE years of building, the ranch infrastructure was sufficient to support the youth groups who came every summer to work in schools and villages. Beyond the ranch, Honduras Outreach had built four medical clinics to address the acute and chronic health issues among the people. Vaccination rates were approaching 100 percent, and malnutrition was decreasing.

Still, diarrhea, parasites, and respiratory diseases ran rampant through the Agalta Valley. Since the inception of Honduras Outreach, summer groups had been building latrines, chimneys, and cement floors for families. But the two hundred North Americans who came to the ranch each year could not meet the needs in the villages. HOI would have to become a year-round program with more adults working throughout the Agalta Valley.

The board of directors asked Sue Church to serve as executive director, working two days a week so she could maintain her physical therapy practice with her husband, Jim. Sue was at home pondering and praying about the situation one morning while she

The two greatest factors in determining the health of a family are water to the home and the education of the mother.

World Health Organization

was ironing. A plan began to unfold in her mind, and she wrote her thoughts. Soon she had the vision for what would become HOI's Model Village Program.

The basic needs were clear: clean water, removal of cooking smoke from homes, reduced direct contact with the ground where parasites breed, and education. Sue believed that adult North American groups would be willing to go out from the ranch and work with villages to provide these things. She also knew, however, that if the visitors simply gave the Hondurans what they needed, the mission's goal of enabling Hondurans to help themselves would be thwarted. A model village would have to be self-sufficient, and to become self-sufficient, the people would have to develop good work habits.

Sue told the board about her theory, and they wanted to test it as soon as possible. They began asking questions and

praying. Success would rely on selecting the right village, the right North American group, and the right Honduran to coordinate the program. José Mondragón had been promoted to director of the ranch; Sue and other board members consulted with him about the idea.

For several reasons, Las Delicias seemed to be the right village to test the program. Before coming to work at the ranch, Dr. Maria Elena Solano had her office there. Several women in the village had begun making pottery to sell to North American visitors at Paraiso, attempting to improve their standard of living. And because Las Delicias was close to the ranch, the villagers had visited many times; they trusted the ranch staff and the North Americans.

Dr. German Jiminez became the first model village coordinator. A year earlier German, a recent medical school graduate, had

filled in at the ranch clinic while Dr. Maria Elena Solano traveled to the United States for ten weeks of training through Global Health Action. At the end of the ten weeks, the staff and the HOI board knew they had to find a permanent position for German.

"He is the kindest and most caring physician I have ever seen," says board member Fran Lewis, a nurse who has worked at the ranch every year since 1990 and became Health Committee chair in 1994. "A Honduran woman with a young boy came into the clinic with generalized complaints—nothing unusual. She was a shy, quiet woman, even quieter than usual for a Honduran woman. After awhile the boy started crying, and Dr. German asked why he was sad. He said his father had died. Then the woman explained that her husband had died a violent death, and both she and her son broke down in tears. German and I were crying as well. Then German picked up the boy and said, 'Don't worry; I'll be your daddy.' German regularly sought out that boy and made sure he was all right."

Hiring German as coordinator of the model village program filled an immediate need while adding another physician to the staff.

First Presbyterian Church of Meridian, Mississippi, donated money to support Las Delicias as a model village. The church did not send a group to work in the village. In fact, unlike subsequent model villages, groups from several churches worked in Las Delicias. What was confirmed through the experience, however, was that with motivation and instruction, Hondurans would work to improve their own standard of living. Many residents of Las Delicias participated in the building of latrines, concrete floors, chimneys, and a water system to the village.

Ten years of partnership with Rancho el Paraiso has not insulated Las Delicias from hardship. Shortly after the last chimneys were installed, a man known as *El Hombre Malo*—the Bad Man— went to the courthouse in Juticalpa and placed a claim on half the land in the village. The people had lived on the land far longer than was required to claim it as their own under Honduran law. El Hombre Malo was able to convince the authorities, however, that the land belonged to him. Then he went out with a bulldozer and knocked down all the houses on "his" side of the road.

The people across the road invited their neighbors to move in with them, then they asked José Mondragón for assistance. José went to Juticalpa to challenge El Hombre Malo's legal claim, to no avail.

With the support of the HOI board, José then offered the people who had lost their homes free land at Rancho el Paraiso, but they declined. Las Delicias was their home, and they would stay there. So they rebuilt, and El Hombre Malo came back with his bulldozer. They rebuilt again, and as of this writing he has not returned. But the rebuilt homes are among the worst shacks in the Agalta Valley. El Hombre Malo has threatened José with

When we started working in the villages pouring concrete floors, the Honduran women didn't do anything, and the men laughed at us for pouring perfectly good concrete on the ground. Now they outwork us. For us it's more fellowship. For them it's an opportunity for their kids to have a better chance.

Archie Crenshaw

violence against the ranch if anyone on staff helps improve homes on "his" side of the road. José and the board have reminded the people in those homes that their offer still stands—free land and help building nice homes.

DESPITE opening an HOI health clinic in La Ensenada in 1994, the infant mortality rate in the village remained high. The problem was the water. The small stream that served as the village's only source of water did not flow rapidly enough to wash away the waste from the village's one hundred families.

Henry Mencias, then the government health promoter in the area, preached the importance of boiling water. Dr. Lee Woodall, a member of the HOI board's Health Committee, reiterated the message whenever he visited. Finally one mother told another, "Since the gringos came and I started boiling water, my kids don't get sick anymore." Sharing that information unsolicited with friends began to change things, but not fast enough. Children were still dying at an alarming rate.

Lee and José Mondragón went to the Honduran governmental agency that directed USAID money for rural water projects. They hoped to be able to pipe water from farther upstream into a holding tank where it would remain clean. But the agency ran tests on the creek and determined that there was not enough flow to keep the tank filled.

Convinced that a solution existed, Lee spent a week in La Ensenada. He ate every meal in the mayor's home, with José or Dr. German Jiminez coming out from the ranch as well. They brainstormed the water issue around the dining table, and the mayor told them that there were some bold creeks farther up in the mountains.

Lee believed those streams were the answer to La Ensenada's problem. The next day he and José went back to

DR. GERMAN JIMINEZ
AND ELENA MONDRAGÓN
IN THE HEALTH CLINIC

Juticalpa to meet with the water authorities and tell them about the creeks. While they were in the office, a young American named Courtney came in. He was a hydrologist down from New Hampshire doing an internship, and he had conducted the first water study for La Ensenada a month earlier. Courtney said he was leaving in another month.

Lee told him about the streams in the mountains and agreed to pay for a second study if he would come out again. Lee, José, and Courtney all tromped across the mountains and forest, through the coffee fields, to the place where two clear streams came together. Courtney determined that there was plenty of water for the village. Getting it there would be another matter.

The streams were about thirty feet higher than La Ensenada, but there were two ridges and valleys that would have to be crossed, and with only gravity available to move the water, only a well-designed, well-built system would work. The plan called for a four-inch pipe to carry water through the valley and up to a tank on the next ridge, which was about ten feet lower than the stream. Another tank on the next ridge, which was another ten feet lower, held the water temporarily. The final stretch of pipe ran through yet another valley and up to the village holding tank, which was another ten feet lower. From the final tank, pipes would be run to spigots outside each home in the village.

Construction of the system and installation of four kilometers of pipe was not a job North American volunteers could take on. HOI would provide the materials, the design, and help start the project, then the villagers would have to complete the work themselves.

Lee returned the next fall to get started, and it rained all day every day. But with help from José and others from the ranch, the villagers dug out a place in the stream and built a cement trough leading to the pipe.

Many of the villages cannot be reached by bus or van. To get groups to those villages, two military trucks have been bought and donated to the ranch. The first one was a 1972 model and was a great deal for the ranch. It had less than twenty thousand miles on the odometer and had never been dropped from an airplane. The second truck, three years older and a bit more "experienced," proved to be incredibly durable.

The ranch staff was taking a group to the airport in Tegucigalpa. The North Americans rode in buses, and all their luggage was stacked in the back of the truck. When a car came speeding around a mountain toward the truck, the ranch driver swerved to avoid a collision but lost control and went off the road and straight down a hundred-foot drop.

The back of the truck was crushed, but the driver climbed out with just a bump on his shoulder. The engine never stopped running.

When she saw the damage, Sue Church thought the crushed rear end meant the end of the truck, but the staff convinced her that they could fix it. "I don't now how they did it," she says, "but they straightened it out. We have very resourceful people on our staff."

Then the men of La Ensenada took over. Every able-bodied male in the village pledged to work one day a week until the project was finished. That meant working through the hundred-day coffee picking season, and coffee was their only source of cash revenue. They were pledging 14 percent of their annual income—they worked seven days a week during the picking season for a dollar a day—for the sake of clean water.

A year later the mayor of La Ensenada sent word to Lee that they had completed the system, and invited him down for its dedication. Lee and his son, Wright, went down for the celebration. "As part of the celebration," Lee recalls, "a woman walked around with a clay pot on her head, symbolizing all the women who for centuries had gone to the stream with a pot for their water. Then she threw the pot on the ground, smashing it, and cried, 'Never again!'"

In the year following installation of the system, the occurrence
of diarrhea fell from twenty cases a week to only two a month.

When other villages learned of the virtual elimination of
infant mortality from dehydration in La Ensenada, they too wanted
clean water. Honduras Outreach subsequently has supported
construction of water systems throughout the valley.

SPANNING RIVERS

DURING the rainy season, the people of San Martín could not
cross the river to get to school or to the health clinic at Rancho
el Paraiso. In 1994, after the dorm and clinic had been built,
the North Americans rose to the challenge of building a concrete
and steel bridge across the river.

WAYNE MADDUX BRIDGE

Dan Pattillo designed a bridge that would rely on steel ceiling trusses—lots of them—for support. He shipped down the materials that could not be bought in Honduras, using plywood boxes that would be converted into forms for concrete footings. A Rotary Club in Conyers, Georgia, donated a cement mixer that would mix thirteen wheelbarrow loads at a time.

Dan took his crew down to the river, where they built an earthen dam and used four culverts to divert the flow of the water while they built the bridge. The bridge was nearing completion when the rain started. It rained and it rained, and the diverted river washed sticks and entire trees downstream. The trees clogged the culverts, and the water kept coming, washing over the culverts and the temporary dam. When trees slammed into the new bridge, it was only a matter of time before the bridge itself became a dam that could never hold back such a torrent. The concrete buckled, and the bridge was gone before it had ever been used. Discouraged but not dismayed, the North Americans came back and rebuilt the bridge, and it is still in use.

Similarly the group from Honduras Outreach decided to build a bridge across the Rio Grande so the people from El Jobo would not be isolated during the rainy season. But the backhoe they used to dig footers could not dig deep enough for a solid foundation. "While we were building the bridge," Matt Moore recalls, "a man who looks like an elderly John Wayne rode out from the village on his horse. He came over to me and Tony Dowd—Tony was a Department of Transportation engineer. He looked at the river, then at us, and he shook his head. Then he pointed at the sky and made a *whoosh* with his hands.

Washed out two years later, the bridge is still high enough to allow year-round foot traffic, which is what the people had asked for. The only first-time success in bridge building was one built by Mission del Sol Church in Phoenix, Arizona, across the Rio Matadero between Las Delicias and Juan XXIII.

After those experiences, Honduras Outreach decided to build bridges between people, not across rivers.

BRIDGING SOULS

ANYONE who has traveled through the Appalachian Mountains of the eastern United States can quickly grasp the geology of central

Honduras. Green ridgelines and valleys run first this way, then that, some parallel to the next ridge, others abruptly changing directions, creating hundreds of isolated coves and mountaintops where families and small villages live with few outside influences. Honduras has been virtually 100 percent Roman Catholic throughout its history. In their isolation, however, small Protestant congregations out in the mountains have embraced many diverse ways of reaching out to Christ—much like they have in rural Appalachia. In his description of religion for the PBS documentary *The Appalachians,* Howard Dorgan might just as easily have been describing religion in central Honduras:

> Baptist subsets alone can number into the seventies or eighties, depending on how narrowly the divisions are drawn. . . . In addition, Pentecostals and Holiness-Pentecostals challenge the Baptists with their own lengthy continuum of persuasions, particularly the small independent congregations that gather in homes, abandoned storefronts, or backcountry wood-frame structures, displaying cryptic titles such as the Foursquare Holiness-Pentecostal Church of Miracles, Signs, and Wonders. In short, these mountains are home to a complex patchwork of Christian faiths.

Few of the pastors of these community churches of Honduras have been educated beyond sixth grade, and almost none of them have any formal training to support them in their calling. They rely heavily on the Holy Spirit to direct them in their preaching and their church administration.

The growth of Protestant denominations through the 1980s and '90s led to rivalries with the Catholic Church and

The delay in finding a ranch pastor and training materials might have made the HOI ministry more effective in the long run. It gave the ministry an opportunity to earn the people's trust before talking to them about their faith.

"Health was the fastest thing we could do to get people to trust us," Sue Church says. "Once they trusted us to that degree, they were willing to go to the next step, which was education. So while it was unfortunate that we didn't find anybody to lead our Christian teaching ministry early on, I'm not sure that it slowed us down in that area."

then among various Protestant congregations. Pastors called members of their congregations "brother" and "sister," but they hardly spoke to those outside their flocks. The epitome of this attitude, Sue Church recalls, was when a little girl died and her next-door neighbor, who was a minister, did not attend her funeral because she was not a member of his congregation.

ROGER and another member of the Church of Christ congregation near the ranch, seeking common ground, organized a unity service among all the pastors in the area and invited Edgardo Guevara, pastor of the Quadrilateral Church in La Venta, to lead it.

Unlike many of the Protestant pastors, Edgardo was considered a "preacher of the people," lacking the judgmental bent seen in some others. Additionally he owned a successful roofing-tile company, so he was respected by many in the poor communities for not relying on congregational gifts for his income.

Sue was at the ranch the week Edgardo led the unity service, and she was so impressed with his message that she invited him to meet with José and her to discuss a Bible Institute that Honduras Outreach hoped to establish. Edgardo brought two of his parishioners with him, and as they discussed the ecumenical nature of the program, one of the men said, "You're not going to allow Catholics to participate, are you?"

Before Sue or José could respond, Edgardo, who understood the potential impact of the program, answered, "You don't understand; this is bigger than any denomination."

There is no distinction between Jew and Greek, for the same Lord over all is rich to all who call upon Him.

Romans 10:12

Honduras Outreach sees in Edgardo and his fellow spiritual leaders the greatest opportunity for expanding God's reach into the Agalta Valley. Local pastors can be much more effective than foreign missionaries, but they need support and training.

IN the mid-1990s, the HOI board began looking for curriculum materials to train the pastors and for someone who could conduct the training. For months they scoured publishers' catalogs and prayed for basic pastoral training written in Spanish. Their prayers were answered at a wedding shower in Decatur.

Dennis Mock was two years out of law school when he executed the legal work for Jerry Eickhoff's first corporation in 1971. Dennis and his wife, Pat, were also members of Decatur First United Methodist Church, where Sue Church taught their children's Sunday school class.

In 1982 Dennis was called to the ministry. He and Pat left Decatur First for Dallas, where Dennis earned his master's degree in biblical studies from Dallas Theological Seminary. They then returned to Georgia, and Dennis joined the staff of First Baptist Church, Atlanta.

Dennis and Jerry stayed in touch through the years, although not closely, and when Jerry's daughter Kelly was getting married, Pat Mock attended a wedding shower. She and Sue Church sat beside each other at lunch and spent most of the time talking about their children. When they finally got around to talking about what they had been doing, Pat said that Dennis had been on a mission trip to Kenya a few years earlier and realized that the pastors there had almost no training literature in their own language. He came home with a burden to create such a curriculum and wrote a ten-segment, informal training program for church leadership. Then he created the Bible Training Center for Pastors and Church Leaders, a ministry that translates the curriculum he wrote into other languages and equips trainers to present the material to pastors and church leaders around the world.

Sue just about dropped her fork into her cake. This was exactly what HOI had been looking for. She couldn't wait to see the material and to tell the other HOI board members.

As it turned out, the ministry was located less than a mile from HOI's warehouse east of Atlanta. Jerry invited Dennis to Honduras, where the search for a full-time missionary who would live at the ranch and train pastors from nearby villages had been long and difficult. No one had stepped forth to make the commitment.

As a temporary solution, the ranch had for several years brought in faith leaders to conduct weeklong workshops for pastors, and at one of those workshops someone mentioned Douglas González, a Venezuelan minister, as a possible candidate for the permanent position.

Douglas joined Honduras Outreach in 1998, and a large storage barn was remodeled to house the Louise Mahaffey Bible Training Center for the Americas.

Dennis trained Douglas to teach the Bible training curriculum, then helped recruit the first class of local pastors for the

"Teach [the commandments of the LORD] to your children and your grandchildren, especially concerning the day you stood before the LORD your God at Horeb, when the LORD said to me, 'Gather the people to Me, and I will let them hear My words, that they may learn to fear Me all the days they live on the earth, and that they may teach their children.'"

Deuteronomy 4:9-10

After several years we had finished our work in the village of Coronado and were set to make our first trip to La Jagua, a remote village up in the mountains. We wanted to take gifts to the village on Sunday, our first day, as we had each year in Coronado. But getting all of our people to La Jagua was hard enough; we were told we couldn't take our stuff too. I was so distressed—we had always taken things to people in the village. Then someone said, "God wants us to go in there just as we are. We have nothing. If we go in with our things, they look at our things. So God is sending us in just as we were—just one human being to another."

June Barnett

Bible Training Center. Douglas then led the group through four hundred hours of training in courses that included:

• Bible study methods and rules of interpretation
• Old Testament survey
• New Testament survey
• Communicating biblical messages
• Bible doctrine survey
• Personal spiritual life
• Church ministry/administration/education
• Missions/evangelism/discipleship

When his first class of pastors gathered together in the Bible Training Center, Douglas he told them, "Leave your denominations at the door. This is not about your denomination. This is about understanding faith."

MANY of the villages in the Agalta Valley and surrounding mountains remain extremely isolated and difficult to serve. The nurse in HOI's health clinic at Las Manzanas has eight villages she can reach only by horseback. Realizing the importance of access to health care, a village gave the nurse a horse to use when she needs it.

Other villages the ranch serves cannot be reached by vehicle during the rainy season. Groups can work in those villages only in February. And still others are so far from the ranch that the groups working there stay in a nearby health clinic at night rather than coming all the way back every day.

"We try to put groups where it's not too far outside their comfort zone," Sue Church says. "But some groups don't like staying at the ranch. It's too civilized for them, and they prefer living and working farther out when they're in Honduras."

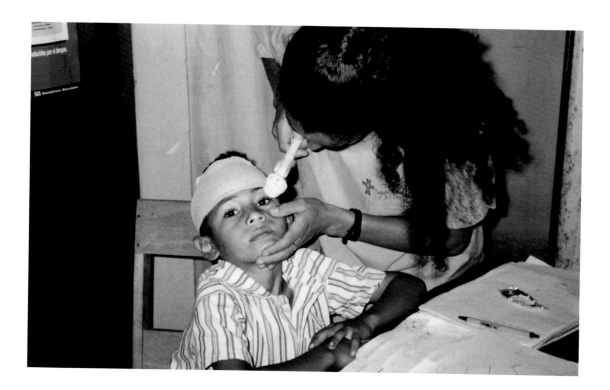

THE people Honduras Outreach serves, and most of the local
people who work at the ranch, never learned to make a decision.
North Americans grow up making choices, but poor Hondurans
don't have that opportunity. They eat one thing. They have one or
two sets of clothes, and they wear whatever is clean.

"So the foundation of everything we've done for the staff,"
Sue says, "is to teach them it's okay to make a decision."

Shortly after Sue became executive director of
Honduras Outreach, she began training the staff to make
choices and to be less reliant on North Americans to make
decisions for them. She knew there might come a time when
the ability to make a decision might be the difference
between life or death.

"I started out by asking them their favorite color," she
recalls, "and nobody would tell me. Instead they asked what
my favorite color was. They were afraid to answer because

their favorite might not be my favorite. But I wouldn't answer until they answered first. They were learning to express their own opinions.

"We went from there to increasingly harder situations, and I asked them why they had such a hard time choosing. They said, 'Because we are always told what to do.'

"In Honduras, for the most part, the boss knows everything, and the employee knows only his or her little part. You don't know how your part relates with other people. I was teaching them how to assess their own needs, create priorities, and make decisions based on that information."

The need for training became clear later when Sue asked Ubaldo Ponce to become a group assistant. Ubaldo loved to drive, loved to joke with the North Americans, and loved to go to Tegucigalpa; he was a hard worker and was willing to work at

night. But when Sue suggested the possibility of his working with visiting groups, he declined. Sue asked why, and he explained, "If they sent me to the store for watermelon and they didn't have any, I wouldn't know what to do."

Over time, however, the staff grew confident in their decision-making ability and became more independent thinkers. Nine years after Archie, Joe, and Jerry first visited the Agalta Valley, that confidence would prove vital as the people they had come to love faced their greatest test.

CHAPTER 11

HURRICANE MITCH

And the rain descended, the floods came, and the winds blew and beat on that house; and it did not fall, for it was founded on the rock.

Matthew 7:25

THE 1998 hurricane season was almost over when the thirteenth tropical depression of the year formed in the Caribbean Sea near the coast of Colombia. On Thursday, October 22, as twenty members of Tarrytown United Methodist Church in Austin, Texas, prepared for their Saturday departure to Honduras, winds increased and the depression became tropical storm Mitch. Forecasters expected Mitch to move north toward Jamaica as it continued to strengthen.

The folks from Texas didn't give the storm a second thought as they boarded their plane on Saturday morning. Anyone who checked the Weather Channel that morning would have seen that Mitch was still moving due north toward Jamaica, Cuba, and Florida. Forecasters expected it to slowly turn west toward the Yucatan Peninsula, putting it at least two hundred miles north of Honduras.

At Rancho el Paraiso, José Mondragón had not heard about Mitch. All of his news came from the newspapers he picked up whenever he was

in San Esteban, and the papers were not yet reporting on the storm brewing five hundred miles to the east. On Saturday morning he took a group to the airport and waited for the group from Texas to arrive a few hours later. While waiting he made his weekly call to Sue Church in the States.

Knowing José had no way of keeping up with storms at sea, Sue tracked the progress of every tropical depression in the Caribbean, whether or not they appeared to threaten Honduras. All week she had been watching the depression that became Mitch, and she told José, "It looks like it's not coming your way, but we need to keep an eye on it." She asked José to call her on Monday morning in case the storm moved closer to Honduras. José would have to drive into San Esteban to place the call.

IN three previous trips to Rancho el Paraiso, groups from Tarrytown United Methodist Church in Austin, Texas, had worked extensively in the village of El Jobo, installing concrete floors in homes, building latrines and chimneys, and installing drainage lines to remove standing water from the village.

The Texans had also rehabilitated a building just outside the ranch gate that had once been used as an orphanage. Now it was a kindergarten. Inspired by the possibilities and the need for education throughout the Agalta Valley, the Tarrytown group had brought woodworking equipment to the ranch and begun an ongoing project to build desks and chairs for

LOADING KINDERGARTEN FURNITURE

children and teachers in the kindergartens supported by Honduras Outreach.

When they went to work on the last week of October 1998, the group split into three teams. One team stayed at the ranch and built furniture, another helped build a library in the nearby village of Dos Rios, and a medical team assisted in HOI-funded health clinics across the Agalta Valley. There had been rain when the group arrived on Sunday, but on Monday and Tuesday the weather was typically warm and breezy.

Sue told José when he called on Monday that Mitch had veered farther south, but National Weather Service computer models still indicated a turn to the north, away from Honduras. She asked him to call again on Tuesday.

By Tuesday morning, the storm still had not turned north. Sue and José discussed a possible evacuation of the ranch and decided, based on forecasters' predictions of a northward track, to give it one more day.

Tuesday evening, as the Austin group relaxed in rocking chairs on the porch after supper, the wind grew continually stronger. They couldn't feel the full force of it because it was blowing from out of the north, from behind the dorm. But the huge guanacaste tree in front of the dorm creaked and groaned as the wind roared through it. One man remarked that it sounded like a 747 taking off, and another recalled a sixty-five-mile-an-hour norther back in Texas and said this one seemed much stronger.

Somewhat unnerved, they went to bed and listened to the wind through the night as it pelted the roof with small limbs. Then one of the clay roof tiles banged hard. Every North American lay awake. Any wind strong enough to lift those heavy tiles could do even more significant damage. For the folks from Texas, it seemed each time they fell asleep, another tile would bang.

By Wednesday morning several bands of heavy rain had swept through, but when the sun rose over the Sierra de Agalta mountains, the wind had calmed and skies were clear. Another beautiful morning in Honduras. The yard was strewn with limbs and roof tiles, but nothing had been damaged significantly. The North Americans had their breakfast and devotional and went to work.

Sue awoke on Wednesday to bad news—and an explanation for the wind the ranch had experienced overnight. Mitch had intensified to a Category Five storm, and with gusts of more than two hundred miles an hour, it had become one of the strongest hurricanes ever recorded. Instead of turning toward the Yucatan Peninsula, Mitch had turned south overnight, directly toward the Honduran coast, and had stopped twenty-five miles offshore. The storm was hammering the Bay Islands and the coastal cities with wind and torrential rains. Forecasters were still predicting a turn back to the northwest and landfall in Belize, but Sue knew the Austin group had to get out

HURRICANE MITCH ON TUESDAY MORNING

today. If the forecasters were wrong and the storm continued south, the staff would have its hands full taking care of villages and their own families. They did not need the added responsibility of twenty North Americans.

José drove to San Esteban to call Sue for an update on the storm. On the northeastern horizon the solid line of high, billowy clouds made him uneasy. He didn't know what the Weather Channel was telling Sue, but Tuesday night's wind and this morning's skies were telling him to get the Americans off the ranch.

The telephones in San Esteban were out, as they often were after a night of rain and wind. José got back in his truck and headed west to the next nearest phone—two and a half hours away in Juticalpa. The drive took him past the ranch again. He approached the ranch entrance, dodging potholes filled with muddy water from Tuesday night's rain, and he was tempted to

turn in and tell the North Americans to pack up—the storm was threatening. He knew that by the time he drove to Juticalpa and back, it would be two o'clock in the afternoon. Assuming that Sue concurred with his assessment, the group would be lucky to get packed, loaded, and back to the hotel in Juticalpa by night-fall. José's gut told him to get the Americans out right now.

He ignored his instincts and drove on past the ranch and through Culuco, Santa Rita, and a dozen other valley villages. A light drizzle fell as he headed up toward the first mountain pass, and soon the drizzle turned to heavy rain. José was thinking he should turn around and go back to the ranch when he rounded a steep bend and saw a mudslide that covered half the road. He had room to pass, but he knew conditions at the higher eleva-tions could be worse. He turned his truck around and drove back to the ranch. As he drove, he formulated his plan. He could get the group into two vans and their bags on a truck. If other mudslides were worse than the one he had just seen, they would never get through, so he would have Nelson Zelaya lead the way on the tractor with chains to pull the vehicles through. He would also pack every shovel he could find and chainsaws in case trees had fallen across the road.

The rain stopped as José turned into the ranch entrance, and he knew he would be disappointing the group from Austin. Their work was barely half completed, and they would not want to leave. He was glad that Stuart Garner and Jim Morriss, members of the HOI board, were part of the group. Since he had not been able to contact Sue, their authority would add weight to José's decision.

At ten o'clock José found Jim building school furniture. He took him aside and explained the situation—the hurricane in the Caribbean, the rain in the mountains, and the mudslide. Jim agreed with José's assessment and his decision.

"When they come in for lunch," Jim said, "we'll tell them to pack up."

"No," José said. "We need to pack up right now."

José sent a messenger over to Dos Rios to bring back the group, and he and Jim broke the news to them. As anticipated, they were disappointed and questioning, but within an hour they were packed and ready to leave.

By noon Sue had not heard from José. Her first thought was that the telephones were probably out in San Esteban and that José was driving to Juticalpa. She prayed that he would call soon. If the storm continued south, the staff might have only a few hours to get the group out before mudslides closed the road through the mountains. She anxiously waited for José's call, but she wouldn't hear his voice again for over a week.

RAIN was just beginning at the ranch when the vans pulled away from the dorm. Nelson had gotten a head start on the tractor so

the faster vehicles wouldn't have to creep alongside him. He was waiting at the first mudslide, the one that had convinced José to evacuate. Ubaldo Ponce, who was driving one of the vans, got out and attached a chain from the tractor to his van, and Nelson pulled it through the mud. They repeated the process with the other van and the pickup truck carrying luggage, shovels, and chainsaws, and they were on their way again.

At the next mudslide several other vehicles were stuck. Nelson pulled them out before pulling the vans through the mud. Then, near the top of the next peak, the entire mountainside appeared to lie across the road. José, Nelson, Ubaldo, and group leader Marvin Bettencourth took shovels from the pickup and started shoveling mud. Several of the men from Austin grabbed shovels and helped. When they hit tree trunks buried in the mud, Ubaldo and Nelson pulled out the chainsaws. They couldn't see the trees under the mud, which had oozed back almost as quickly as they had shoveled it away, so they had to cut by feel. After more than an hour they had cleared a narrow path through the mud and tree trunks. Nelson hopped up on the tractor and pulled the vans and pickup truck through.

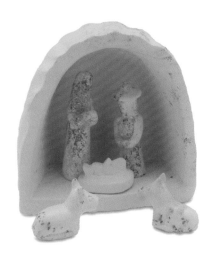

At the next mudslide several people stood looking at the mess and wondering how they might get their vehicles through. A man in a pickup truck, with his wife and their baby at his side, gunned the accelerator forward and back digging himself deeper into the muck until the truck was mired up to the chassis. When he finally gave up, Ubaldo waded through the mud and attached the chain to the truck. But when Nelson began pulling with the tractor, the giant wheels could not get enough traction to get the truck out. It was too deep in the mud. After several attempts, they gave up and the family abandoned their truck. They stood and watched helplessly as Ubaldo hooked the vans to the tractor. Nelson soon realized, though, that the mud

was too deep and soft to pull the vans filled with people. So the group from Austin got out and waded through the knee-deep muck, then stood on the other side with the Honduran family as the tractor pulled the vehicles through. Another Honduran driver whom Nelson pulled through promised to take the stranded family to safety. The North Americans were bidding them farewell when the side of the hill caved in and swept away the abandoned pickup truck in the mud. The group fell silent, considering what might have happened and thanking God for His protection.

The remainder of the trip was slow but less eventful. The North Americans crossed the bridge over the roaring Juticalpa River and arrived in Juticalpa at 9:30 p.m. A drive that normally took two-and-a-half hours had taken more than eight. Every street in Juticalpa was a shallow river, and telephones were out all over town, so José could not call the United States with news. They checked into the Hotel Honduras and awoke Thursday morning to learn that the Juticalpa River bridge had been washed out overnight. If José had not insisted that they

NATIONAL GEOGRAPHIC COVERAGE OF HURRICANE MITCH

leave when they did, they would now be on the wrong side of the river. As the group looked forward to arriving in Tegucigalpa and getting on a plane bound north, they wondered how José and the other ranch staff would get home.

The road from Juticalpa to Tegucigalpa was paved, so the tractor was no longer needed. Nelson drove it to San Francisco de la Paz, where he could drive no farther. He started walking toward home—and toward the hurricane, which was just coming ashore seventy miles northeast of the ranch.

AFTER another daylong drive through the mountains, José led the Austin group into Tegucigalpa at dusk on Thursday, and they checked into the Maya Hotel. The airport was closed. From their rooms they watched disaster below as the already raging Choluteca River swept away entire barrios that had been built against its shores.

On Friday morning José told the group that Ubaldo and he

HIGHWAY NEAR TRUJILLO IN NATIONAL GEOGRAPHIC

were going to try to get home to their families. The hotel was safe, and Marvin, who was single, would stay with them until they could get on a plane back to the States. By that time, however, the bridge over the Rio Hondo had washed out and some men had rigged a cable across the water. José and Ubaldo got into a boat, grabbed the cable, and pulled themselves across the water. Then they walked all day to a spot where they met Ubaldo's brother, who took them to Juticalpa. It would be several more days before they could get the rest of the way home.

The brunt of the storm finally hit Tegucigalpa, dumping rain by the foot. In the midst of the hurricane, the Texans went to work. They located a Red Cross shelter and found work to do in the kitchen, preparing twenty-five thousand meals for people left homeless by the storm. They also sorted donated clothes for those who had nothing. Back at the hotel they worked in the laundry room because the staff was unable to get to work. All this while they waited for the airport to reopen.

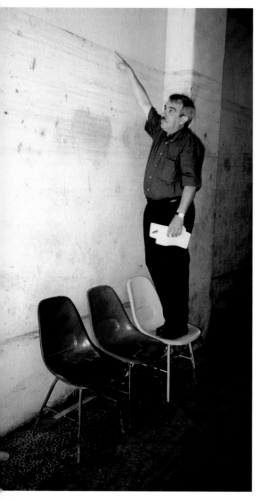

DR. NERY MADRID
NOTES HIGH-WATER MARK

BY Monday morning Sue still had not heard anything from Honduras. CNN was her only source of news, and nothing looked good. Fifty inches of rain had fallen over two days across the country. "We have before us a panorama of death, desolation, and ruin in all of the national territory," President Carlos Flores Facusse said in a nationally broadcast speech.

HOI board members and friends met at the headquarters on Monday morning to pray and to plan a response to Mitch. They knew the country would need food, clothes, building materials, tools, and bottled water, and they began making arrangements to collect those things for shipping. They created ad hoc committees to coordinate fund-raising, communications, and shipping. They also cancelled all group trips to the ranch for the rest of the year.

Coincidentally, Sue had shipped a container of supplies to the ranch, and the ship had sailed from Gulfport, Mississippi, one week before the storm hit. That shipment would be one of the first to arrive in Honduras in the wake of Mitch.

Finally, late Monday afternoon, Sue received an e-mail from Robert Durkee, one of the group leaders from Austin. The country was devastated, he wrote, but the group was well, as were José, Nelson, Ubaldo, and Marvin. Breathing a sigh of relief and a prayer of thanksgiving, Sue forwarded the information to all of the HOI board members. On Wednesday the Austin group was finally able to leave the country.

THERE was still no way of getting a message to or from the ranch. More than a week after the rain stopped, the Juticalpa River finally returned to its banks, and vehicles could ford the stream and drive east toward Trujillo. The Juticalpa-to-Trujillo bus began its daily route again, going as far as the first mudslide and then returning to Juticalpa.

Juan Pablo Aquilera, the accountant at
Rancho el Paraiso, lived in Juticalpa and had
been at home when the storm hit. Desperate for
news from the ranch, each morning he gave a
piece of paper to the bus driver and asked him to
note how far down the road he could go before
having to turn back. When he could make it to
Culuco, the village on the main road at the
entrance to the ranch, he asked him to have
someone from the staff tell him how things were.

FLOOD-SOAKED MEDICAL RECORDS

Like the dove Moses sent from the ark,
the driver made it farther down the road each
day. Then one day he came to Juan Pablo's door with a note.
He had made it to Culuco, and he had returned with a message from the ranch. Juan Pablo immediately faxed the note to
HOI headquarters.

⌒

The best place in all the world to be is Rancho el Paraiso.
We are safe. The people are all working together. We are
providing the people with food and water. We love you,
but do not come now. We can organize our needs, and
you can be there to help get us the things we need so we
can get back on our feet.

⌒

DETAILS of the devastation wrought by Mitch were overwhelming.
The homes of nearly 1.4 million people were destroyed. The Aguan
River, usually the width of a football field, had cut a path of
destruction ten miles wide through the state of Colón. Two-thirds of
the country's bridges and much of the highway system were wiped
out. In a country with a national budget of $1.1 billion, damage
from the hurricane was calculated at more than $5 billion. A

NELSON ZEYALA, MARY FLAKE DE FLORES, AND UBALDO PONCE

Honduran Chamber of Commerce official told *National Geographic* magazine, "The math is simple. If we don't get help from abroad over the next ten years, it will take generations to get back to where we were."

Honduran First Lady Mary Flake de Flores coordinated the relief effort, creating the Maria Foundation to direct international humanitarian aid. All shipments into the country had to be coordinated through the Maria Foundation—all except those of Honduras Outreach. Since meeting Sue Church in February, Señora Flores had watched with interest the work of Honduras Outreach in the rural eastern portions of her country. She was confident that HOI could manage relief efforts in those rural eastern areas while she and the Maria Foundation concentrated on the heavily populated urban regions of Honduras. She asked that HOI keep the foundation informed of its efforts and shipments of goods and materials into the country, but otherwise gave Honduras Outreach broad authority to evaluate and respond to needs.

In Atlanta the HOI warehouse became a center of constant activity. Prior to Mitch, two containers per year had been shipped to the ranch. Now a full-time coordinator received goods and built containers through the week, and thirty volunteers came in every Saturday to build more containers, pack them, and ship them by truck to Gulfport, Mississippi. HOI sent four containers every Saturday. Two weeks later those containers would arrive at the ranch. Sue expanded her work schedule to five days a week to coordinate the effort.

The Hispanic communities in Atlanta and Tennessee responded immediately and generously. "The only problem was they were stronger than our volunteers, so we had to ask them to pack their things in smaller boxes so we could move them around," Sue recalls.

THE Rancho el Paraiso staff has a Christmas party every December, and several North Americans—HOI board members and other supporters—usually go down. They longed to see the people they loved so much, to hug them and hold their hands and encourage them in their time of tragedy. But five weeks after Mitch, with food in Honduras scarce and the ranch staff spending so much time rebuilding, Sue, Jerry, and others believed it was a bad time to go down.

"We don't need to be eating the little bit of food you have," Sue explained to José.

José insisted that they come anyway. "We need to see you and to touch you as much as you need to see and touch us," José said. And with that, Sue knew she was going. The ranch staff asked that eight North Americans come down, and all eight of them did: Sue; Jerry Eickhoff; Meg Lewis, U.S. group coordinator; Fred Ingle, agriculture committee chair; Lee Woodall; Lisa Arledge, scholarship program administrator; and Jim and Annett Morriss, members of the Austin group. They took everything they would need for a Christmas fiesta.

José and Ubaldo were at the baggage claim area, and when the eight came through the door, Sue recalls, "We just fell on each other. That's the only way to describe it." When the tears stopped flowing, they loaded into trucks for the ride to the ranch.

José said it was the first time since the hurricane they had been able to make the entire trip without someone having to pull a truck through at least one mudslide.

When Jose insisted that HOI board members come to Honduras for the Christmas party, he was thinking of more than just the staff who wanted to see their North American friends. He knew that many people throughout the Agalta Valley needed to see that their friends would be back to help them through the disaster. When they learned of the arrival of the eight board members, dozens of those people came to see them.

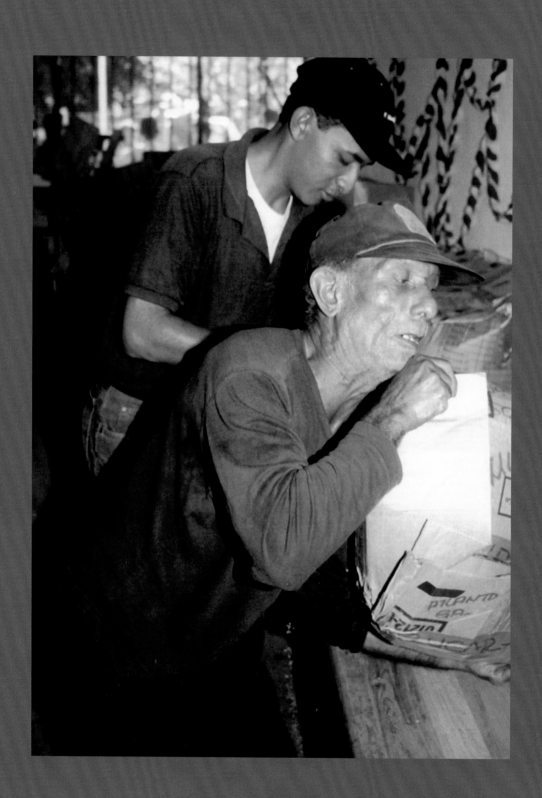

CHAPTER 12

REBUILDING

Restore us, O God; cause Your face to shine, and we shall be saved!

Psalm 80:3

THE DEVASTATION from Tegucigalpa to Rancho el Paraiso was monumental. Miles of paved road were washed out. Bridges were gone and rivers had to be forded. Every house that had once had a thatch roof was open. Mounds of mud indicated where homes had once stood, and groups of mounds indicated villages. People everywhere seemed to move in slow motion.

Not so in the Agalta Valley. Two weeks after the storm had passed, all of the villages had sent damage assessments to the ranch. Almost all of the damage had been caused by water, not wind, and villagers were working together to rebuild. They had the materials at hand to replace mud huts with thatch, but they would need continuing shipments of food; their fields had been destroyed.

At the ranch damage to structures had been minimal, but five thousand trees had been lost. Before the storm had hit full force, the staff had harvested all of the chickens. The cattle were on high ground, and they all survived.

Several containers of food and material were lined up in front of the hacienda when the group arrived at the ranch for the Christmas party. José explained that all of the villages the ranch served had received what they needed for that week, and some was left over. Realizing that the full containers created an unnecessary temptation, he suggested that they be shared with villages beyond Rancho el Paraiso's normal reach. So the next morning he and the North Americans took a load to Las Avisbas. The residents of the little village stood around their battered homes hungry and despondent a month after the hurricane had come and gone. Many of them had pinkeye and other evidence of unsanitary conditions, and the river running past the village was still filled with debris from the storm.

The people of Las Avisbas had obviously done nothing since the storm but wait for help. José explained that they were bringing food for them to divide among themselves.

"You have to divide it for us," the villagers said. "We can't decide."

"But you know who needs what," José said. "We don't."

Still the people insisted that they could not decide—that they would just start fighting over things.

"Then what you must do," José said, "is create a council of nine people who will determine who needs what, and they will distribute everything. And if I hear of you arguing over anything, we won't bring any more."

Then José told them they would have to clean the debris from the river before he would bring anything else.

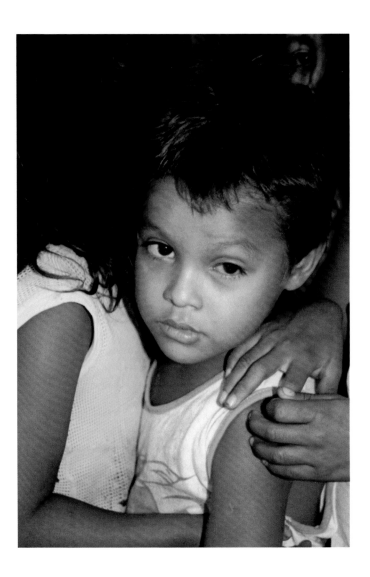

The sad state of the people of Las Avisbas confirmed a realization that had been growing throughout José's report on the other villages. Ten years earlier, people throughout the Agalta Valley villages would have responded to tragedy just as this village had. But through years of interactions with Rancho el Paraiso staff, who insisted that they work together to improve their own conditions, they were becoming independent and able to take care of themselves.

REBUILDING and supplying operations had gone smoothly for several weeks, then in December the port in Honduras became a logjam of containers from North America. Many well-meaning churches and charities were sending cargo to the country without making arrangements for a consignee to sign for the shipment at the Honduran port. By law no container could leave

the Honduran port to go inland until it had been correctly received. For several weeks in early 1999, shipments to the ranch slowed to a trickle.

Finally in February the logjam at the port broke, and ships were able to offload their cargo. Within days the ranch had seventy shipping crates—the equivalent of about ten tractor-trailer loads—filled with food and supplies. José devised a plan for moving things out quickly. He went to San Esteban and to smaller villages the ranch served and explained that they could come and get what they needed, but first they had to complete a community work project to help them move beyond the disaster. They might be required to remove stumps from a river, for example. A local authority would then have to certify that the work had been done before the goods would be released.

On the morning that the people of San Esteban were scheduled to receive their provisions, cattle trucks were lined up two by two all the way from the hacienda to the clinic. Sue, who was down for the first time since December, guessed that as many as five hundred people had shown up.

José and German were coordinating the ranch staff as they prepared to begin distribution when a physician from San Esteban walked up to José. He explained that the people had not completed their work projects, but the mayor of San Esteban had certified them anyway.

José knew what had to be done, and he briefly discussed the matter with German. Then the three men—José, German, and the physician from San Esteban—told the crowd they could not get their provisions. They would have to go home and honor their commitment first.

In a crowd that large there were sure to be people with guns, and trouble could erupt in a hurry. But the people did not protest. They just got in their trucks and cars and went home.

Except for one old blind woman who was led over to Sue Church.

"But I'm poor," the woman said, "and I can't work."

Sue wanted to help the woman—to give her something—but she had seen the powerful positive effect of insisting that the people work before receiving.

"Can you make tortillas?" she asked the woman.

"Yes," she said.

"Then you go home and make tortillas for the workers and then come back." The woman went away.

The mayor of San Esteban came to the ranch later that day and apologized for the trouble he had created. José told him that he had asked another man in town to certify all the work to be done from that point forward, and a few days later the people of San Esteban returned to the ranch for their supplies.

EVERY day the telephone at the HOI office rang with offers to help the people of Honduras. Carey Odom, owner of a hardware store in Duluth, Georgia, donated $36,000 in building materials and tools, and the North Georgia Conference of the United Methodist Church donated $50,000. In all, HOI received $850,000 in aid for Honduras and shipped six hundred tons of food and material, much more than they could use in the Agalta Valley. So the ranch staff contacted Governor Marion Crispo of Colón, a state that includes the seaport of Trujillo, and offered to share goods for relief. She was grateful and began passing out supplies to the people of Colón. HOI shipped enough beans, corn, rice, and water to feed seventeen thousand people for six months.

Governor Crispo also asked if Honduras Outreach could help in their rebuilding effort. When Sue went down in February 1999, roads had been repaired enough for José and her to meet with the governor and see some of the damage in Colón. Flood damage along the rivers in that department had been far more extensive than in the Agalta Valley. The Aguan River had drowned thousands as it swept away entire villages.

RIDING with Governor Crispo, they passed near what had been the village of Marañones. Although no villagers had been killed, every home had been destroyed. At a high spot along the road, the sixty families of Marañones lived under makeshift shelters of sticks and clear plastic sheets that HOI had used to wrap the emergency supply shipments. At the highest point in their tent village, they flew a Honduran flag atop a long limb. The governor explained that the plastic was a housing upgrade for the people of Marañones. For weeks they had lived under sticks and palm fronds.

They stopped to talk with the people, and when the governor explained that José and Sue were from Honduras Outreach, the people thanked them profusely for sending them the plastic. But they didn't ask for anything else.

"We must help them rebuild their village," José said.

The HOI board agreed to extend the reach of the ranch and send groups into Colón to help rebuild, beginning with Marañones. Governor Crispo found land on higher ground that was controlled in part by the Honduras Department of Defense, which agreed to give several acres to the people of Marañones. Logistics would be difficult. They would have to find temporary housing and hire additional staff to support the Americans, who would have been a four-and-a-half-hour drive from Rancho el Paraiso before the hurricane.

In May, Sue, José, and Governor Crispo returned to the tent village and found that the people of Marañones had upgraded their living conditions by using HOI shipping crates, heavy blue tarps, and roofing tin. They shared a kitchen and were still sleeping on the ground, and they had made a school for their children under a large open tent. They had plenty of food and water, and they were grateful that José and Sue had returned. Apparently others had promised to help but had not yet come back.

Back in the States Meg Lewis began coordinating from HOI headquarters with groups eager to help rebuild. Churches were committed to sending groups to Marañones.

José needed a group coordinator to oversee the project, and Governor Crispo suggested Leslie Bobadillo. Leslie lived in two worlds. Her family home was a mud hut among the poorest of the poor in Trujillo. When she was nineteen she earned a two-year

college scholarship to study aquaculture in the United States, then she came home and worked in shrimp farming.

"I am like the apostle Paul," she said. "I can be happy with abundance or lack. I have my own room in the dorm, my own computer, lots of clothes, everything you can think of. When I go home I have no running water in the house. I go to the river to do laundry. I carry my clothes on my head and bring the wet clothes back to the house and wait until the sun dries them."

When Governor Crispo asked Leslie to consider leading North American groups as they rebuilt villages, Leslie said, "Thank you, but I am not capable." She had never worked in construction, and she was a woman—"a girl, actually," she said—in a male-dominated culture.

HONDURAN FIRST LADY WITH NELSON JR.

But the governor, a woman, insisted that Leslie was right for the job. Her knowledge of the language and American culture would allow her to relate easily to the volunteer workers. She could learn construction, and the men would learn to follow her. Try it for three months, she said, and see how it goes. So Leslie met with José and Sue and accepted their offer.

Then one week before construction was to begin, José, Sue, and Leslie drove over to coordinate delivery of materials so that everything would be in place when the North Americans arrived. But the governor had bad news. The Honduran defense department had not released its claim on land identified for rebuilding above the flood plain. The governor said she had been assured that the president would have all the documents signed so that construction could begin on Monday, but José and Sue were concerned. If the transfer did not occur, a group of North Americans would arrive in a week with nothing to do.

They decided to drive to Tegucigalpa to confirm that the transfer would take place. When she arrived in the city, Sue received a message that she should come to the first lady's office. The president's wife explained that a state of emergency had been declared in Honduras. The secretary of defense refused to give the land for the village of Marañones, she said, so her husband had fired him. The refusal to grant the land was not the only reason for the dismissal, she explained. Rather, it was the last straw after a series of other problems.

Although elated by the news, Sue knew that the bureaucratic machinations necessary for transferring title of the land to the people of Marañones could not occur in time to begin work the following week. Other arrangements would have to be made for the group coming down and others who would follow immediately behind them.

On Tuesday morning Sue and José drove back to Marañones—a twelve-hour trip—to tell the people by the side of the road that they would have to wait until the government had land for them.

"They were wonderful," Sue recalls. "They completely understood, and they even offered to help us work in another location so they could learn the skills they would need when it was their turn to have homes."

But there was no other location, and the North Americans would be arriving on Friday. Sue, José, and Leslie drove to Trujillo in search of a solution. Along the way they drove past what had been the village of Higuerales. Like the people of Marañonez, the people of Higuerales lived in makeshift tents by the side of the road. José stopped the truck and they all got out. José located the village leader, who explained that most of the

Honduras Outreach volunteers also helped rebuild eighty-three homes in Trujllo that were destroyed by Hurricane Mitch. The Wesleyan School in Atlanta took a group of high school students to work on the homes, and Raymond Walker, one of the group's adult leaders, watched the transformation of the young people as they worked.

"For young men, it's not cool to be spiritual or to show much emotion or sensitivity," he says. "But in that environment they saw the love of God in a special way that you can't see here in church or through a local ministry. There they opened up and shared in fellowship and were willing to show their vulnerability. That experience can transform young men. That was at the heart of my desire to start a mission program."

Inspired by the trip to Honduras, Wesleyan increased its emphasis on missions, sending two hundred fifty students to missions across the world every year.

men of Higuerales, a village of twenty-three families, worked in a nearby palm-processing factory. Their village was surrounded by a palm plantation.

On the morning the rain began, the seventy children of the village had been in school. The Aguan River rose so fast, their teacher did not have time to get them to high ground. Instead he got all of the children onto the roof of the school, the only concrete-block building in the village. As he got the last child onto the roof, the raging current swept him away. Some of their parents clung to mango trees, others made it to high ground, and some were lost. Every one of the village's mud huts was swept away.

For three days the children sat on the roof of their schools as livestock and people who had drowned were swept past. Rescuers tried to reach them, but even in a boat with a seventy-five-horsepower motor, they could not navigate the swift current. Finally the waters receded, and the children were rescued. But everything their families had was gone, as was the entire palm plantation.

The Higuerales village leader explained that the owner of the palm plantation had traded higher ground for the land in their village, giving the villagers a similar size tract some distance away for them to rebuild.

"We were so happy to trade for higher ground," the village leader explained, "that we helped plant new palm trees where our village had been."

But they had no money and no material to build new homes.

"Is anyone coming to help you?" José asked.

"Many people and groups have promised help," the man said, "but they have not returned."

Sue began to experience the lightness that comes with answered prayer. "God, let this be the place," she prayed silently.

José explained Rancho el Paraiso's system of sweat equity, community organization, and integration, and asked if the people of Higuerales were interested.

"*¡Sí!*" the man insisted. "*¡Sí! ¡Sí!* When will help arrive?"

"Three days," José said.

The people were jubilant. "Then what do we need to do and when do we start?" the village leader asked.

"Start right now bringing sand up from the river," José said. "It will take that long to get enough to begin work."

When the men of the village went to work at the processing plant the next day, the owner was so grateful for the North American help on the way that he let all of his workers take every other week off—with full pay—

to work on their village until it was rebuilt. HOI groups and the people of Higuerales built twenty-three homes in the new village.

IN October 1999 the people of Marañones finally received title to the land for their new village. HOI coordinated with North American groups to rebuild while surveys were done and the community was laid out. The Rotary Club of Duluth, Georgia, raised $60,000 for materials, and construction began on January 15, 2000. The people continued to live on the side of the road until every home in their village was completed. In fact, the families did not even know which homes would be theirs. Instead they worked together with groups from North America to build all the homes and held a drawing after they were completed to determine who would live in which homes.

When Rob Tolley told his Young Life group in Tampa about an opportunity to help rebuild a village in Honduras following Hurricane Mitch, fifteen-year-old Kristin Luttrell felt God's leading, and she couldn't wait to sign up and go. She came home that evening and told her father all about the opportunity. "Can I go?" she asked.

Scott Luttrell, concerned for his daughter's safety in a developing Latin American country, said no.

"Don't answer me now," Kristin said. "Just pray about it."

"All right," Scott said, "I'll pray about it."

Several days later Kristin asked Scott, "Have you prayed about Honduras?"

"I've prayed about it," Scott said, "and I'm really not at peace about it. I'm concerned about your safety. The only way I can get peaceful about it is if I go with you, and I'm not going to Honduras. So I guess the answer is no."

"Then will you pray about your

That way they all were encouraged to do their best work on every home.

The lottery was a great celebration, as families took turns drawing numbers and squealing, "You're my neighbor!" to their friends.

REFLECTING on the successful experience, Leslie Bobadillo says, "God held me all the way through. I did not feel capable, but it was not really me doing it. It was God working. God gave me for that experience a special ability to feel older when I was with older people and young when I was with younger people, so I related to all of the groups that came."

She says the rebuilding process has changed the outlook of many of her fellow Hondurans. Working through the destruction left by Mitch gave the people a new sense of hope, even those who lost everything. "You have to remember," she says, "I don't have a lot, and if it's gone, I won't be crying for too long. It's not as hard for a poor person to lose everything as it is for a rich person."

When Hurricane Mitch took so much from so many, there was no looking back for them. "There was a spirit of hope," Leslie says, "looking at the future, not looking back. God joins his people coming from all different places—people from North America who had never worked in construction, people who had never left their country before were coming down to help us. That was a blessing to us."

A CALL TO ACTION

John Ellett was at home in Austin, Texas, watching *Nightline* coverage of Hurricane Mitch in Honduras and feeling as if he ought to do something to help—something tangible. But what? John was CEO of a marketing consulting firm, had never visited

Honduras, and knew little about Central America. He could write a check, but that wasn't enough. He was reminded of an article from another time and place by a man who had seen a tremendous need and wrote, "It was something I couldn't *not* do." That was John's sense as he watched the suffering in Honduras. He couldn't not do something. He *had* to do something. God was calling him to get involved directly.

He called a woman at his church who had coordinated local projects for Habitat for Humanity and asked her where to start. She suggested that John call a friend of hers at Tarrytown United Methodist Church, and her friend directed him to Jim Morriss, who was on the board of Honduras Outreach and had been in Honduras during the hurricane.

"I can't be the only person in Austin who wants to do something," John told Jim. "If we can find one community where our involvement would make a difference, especially a community that's not at the top of the priority list for other organizations—one that might otherwise fall through the cracks—we could make a noticeable impact."

Jim agreed and said he was going down to the ranch in February. Perhaps John could accompany him. They would be traveling through Juticalpa, where a hundred or more families along the Juticalpa River had lost their homes. The task of rebuilding would not be overwhelming for a committed North American group, but it would be a significant undertaking. At the same time, with much of the attention in Honduras focused on rebuilding coastal areas, work in Juticalpa might otherwise be delayed.

John thought Juticalpa might attract help from home because, like Austin, it was a capital city, and because folks from Austin traveling to Rancho el Paraiso had spent the night in Juticalpa on their way to the mission.

going to Honduras?" Kristin asked. "Don't answer me now. Just pray about it."

"I'll pray about it," Scott said, "but don't count on anything."

Kristin patiently allowed two weeks to pass before she went back to her father. She gently reminded him of his commitment to pray, and he said he had been doing just that, but he still didn't have a clear answer. Then as they continued talking, he said, "I never thought I would be saying this, but let's go."

Kristin and Scott helped rebuild the village of Higuerales, and the spiritual experience was so moving, Scott has taken his entire family to work in Honduras several times since. By the time she started college in 2002, Kristin had made four trips. When the Tampa City Council commended her for her work, she said, "I consider all the service I've done to be God's blessings. I'm not the one who deserves applause."

John took a video camera to Juticalpa in February to bring back images of the devastation. But there was nothing to show. Flooding along the river had been so severe, all evidence of homes had been washed away. So he focused on the people, whose courage, friendliness, positive outlook, and appreciation for John's interest in their well-being touched him deeply.

Back in Texas John and Jim appeared on a local news show that Dick Rathgeber watched. Dick contacted Jim and asked if he was the same Jim Morriss he had served in the army with thirty years earlier. He was, and Dick, a developer and philanthropist, was soon on board as well.

By April 1999, John, Jim, and Dick had created Austin Helps Honduras and recruited a group to rebuild homes in Juticalpa.

"One of the things we didn't want to do was recreate systems or organizations already in place," John says. "We would partner with those who knew what they were doing—people in the community who knew what needed to be done. We were not going to be a bunch of gringos showing up to do whatever we wanted. Following that strategy, we partnered with two critical organizations: Honduras Outreach, which knew how to connect interest in the United States with action in Honduras, and the Rotary Club of Juticalpa, which was a civic-minded organization of local business professionals in the community."

Knowing the families could not rebuild next to the river, a businessperson in Juticalpa donated land for the people. Over the next couple of years, Austin Helps Honduras worked with the people of Juticalpa to build more than one hundred homes, plus water and sewage systems, electrical service, and a kindergarten. A scholarship program was created to support thirty students through the completion of high school, and construction of an elementary school is in the works.

"Miracles are possible when someone listens to God's call and responds," John says. "It's reassuring that this kind of thing can happen for many people, not just for one. My experience in Honduras has given me a stronger confidence and faith in what is possible."

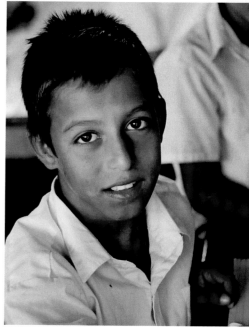

CHAPTER 13

A NEW CREATION

If anyone is in Christ, he is a new creation; old things have passed away; behold, all things have become new.

2 Corinthians 5:17

SOME VILLAGES helped by Honduras Outreach experience seemingly overnight transformations. Others change more slowly. Few villages have changed more dramatically than Culuco, the nearest neighbor to the ranch, and few were more resistant to change.

Culuco's history with the ranch goes back to 1990, when Marco Fonseca took four visitors to the muddy village. When Honduras Outreach created the model village program four years before Hurricane Mitch hit, Culuco was placed at the top of the list of candidates because of its proximity to the ranch. But to become a model village, the people of a village must acknowledge that they want assistance. The people of Culuco refused to ask for help. They just wanted to be left alone.

Then one day Taco, the cantina owner, came face-to-face with God, and he knew he was being called to preach. He closed the cantina and replaced it with a

church. About the same time, two women from Culuco began working at Rancho el Paraiso, one in the kindergarten and the other in the kitchen, and they heard stories of the transformation of villages around the valley.

About that time Jim Thompson invited Methodist Bishop Lindsey Davis and his wife, Jennifer, to visit Rancho el Paraiso. The Davises fell in love with the area and the people, and Jennifer knew she wanted to bring young people from the North Georgia Conference down to this experience. She and Sue Church spent a day visiting villages where the youth might work, but Jennifer, concerned for the children's safety, said she wanted to keep the young people close to the ranch if possible.

What about Culuco? Sue thought. It was a long shot, but it couldn't hurt to ask.

Jennifer walked over to the village with Sue, and the sights and smells nearly overwhelmed her. Culuco had looked a mess from the vehicle, but up close the garbage and the smell of animal and human waste was almost sickening. Several villagers

eyed them suspiciously as Sue asked where they might find
Taco. They found him, and Sue explained that Jennifer was the
wife of a Methodist bishop, and she wanted to bring a group of
young people to work in Culuco. Taco smiled and said he
thought his village was ready to experience transformation.

JENNIFER invited youth from United Methodist churches across
North Georgia to join her in Honduras the next year. Although
the children would pay their own way, Jennifer began raising
money to buy the supplies and materials they would need to
help the people of Culuco. She organized a "Hands to Honduras"
auction and asked ministers around the conference to request
donations from members of their congregations. With quality
gifts and a generous crowd at the auction, they might raise as
much as $10,000.

The night of the auction arrived, and the offerings were more
than Jennifer had imagined. People with vacation homes had
donated weekend and weeklong stays. Teenagers and adults
offered work for hire. Celebrities, including Governor Roy Barnes,
offered dinner. And the people bid generously. By the end of the
night, the auction had raised $60,000 for Honduras.

THE following summer, Jennifer Davis led a group of teenagers
to Honduras. Beth Barnwell, assistant to the senior minister at
Mount Pisgah United Methodist Church, helped Jennifer coordinate the trip. It was Beth's first trip to Honduras. The group
arrived at the ranch on Sunday, and Sue suggested that they
worship at Taco's church that evening. The Georgians walked
up the road to Culuco and gathered with villagers in the dark little former cantina. Taco announced the Scripture, put on his
glasses, opened his Bible, and began to read. Although they did
not understand what he was reading, Jennifer and others were

*You lead Bible school for a group
of children, and during craft time they
make a Popsicle-stick cross. I have
three children, and when they make
crafts like that, they're lucky if they
get them to the van. But in Honduras,
you go back to the village a year
later and you walk into a home, and
there's nothing on the wall but a
Popsicle-stick cross. Their sincerity,
their humbleness, and their genuineness
make every trip life changing.*

Rob Tolley

My wife, Vairin, went to Honduras for the first time, and at the end of the week we were dedicating our work to God in a celebration with the village. During the celebration Berta, a woman in the village, tapped Vairin on the shoulder and led her down the path to her house, a traditional Honduran one-room home. She went to a back corner and brought out a white porcelain dove with gold trim and held it out to Vairin, who didn't speak Spanish, but with tears in her eyes she was able to communicate that she couldn't possibly accept what must have been one of Berta's most prized possessions. But Berta insisted. She was giving it in gratitude. Now it is one of Vairin's most prized possessions.

Rob Tolley

struck by Taco's eloquence. She never guessed that he was virtually illiterate—that he selected his text far enough in advance to memorize it. Another man from the village played an old guitar and led the congregation through several songs, and their fervor excited the North American teenagers. Jamie Hudgins, worship leader for the Georgia group, felt the presence of God as the Hondurans lifted His name. When the service ended, he and the kids wanted more. So on Monday morning, rather than have their devotional time around the cross at the ranch, they gathered at the Culuco church for prayer.

Then they went to work, young people from Georgia alongside families from Culuco, mixing concrete and building latrines. Some visited the one-room elementary school, where Jennifer was amazed at the control the teacher had over his pupils. He told them to be quiet, and they were. *If only schools in America were like that*, she thought. *We could learn a lot down here.*

Several North American youth led the Honduran children with crafts and Bible stories. While they were inside, other children stood outside the school, some of them looking in curiously, and Jennifer wondered how many children in Culuco were not being educated. Later she learned that thousands of Honduran children never start school, and thousands more drop out before they enter sixth grade, especially boys, who help with the family income. Jennifer was troubled.

IN the months after they returned from Honduras, Jennifer and others discussed how they could do more for the people of Culuco. Jennifer organized another auction and raised an additional $50,000. Their expenses in the village—cement, concrete blocks, and other building materials—were a tiny fraction of that amount. They now had more than $100,000 in the bank.

When the Georgia youth returned the following summer, Taco again led them and his congregation in Sunday night worship. The North Americans and the Hondurans took turns singing songs, and the people of Culuco, led by the man with the old guitar, sang out stronger than ever. When they finished singing, Jamie felt led to give his guitar to the Honduran man, but remembering that in this place gifts can sometimes be misconstrued by the recipient, Jamie offered to trade guitars. The man accepted the trade with a warm smile.

Then Taco, as he had done each time they had worshiped together, put on his glasses, opened his Bible, and read several verses of text. He closed the Bible and looked at the North Americans, and as tears streamed down his face and theirs, he told them, "We saw you love each other for no reason. Then we saw you love us for no reason. We learned to love you for no reason. Now we love each other."

I was in the village with Tom Vanderhorst, a retired Delta pilot, and one of the people in the village asked me (I speak Spanish) what Tom did. I said, "He flies for an airline."

"What's an airline?" the man asked.

"A big plane like the one we came to Honduras in."

"You didn't come in a boat?" the man asked.

Large commercial jets don't fly over the Agalta Valley, and the only airplanes this man had ever seen were the very small ones that only occasionally fly over. It hit me then how isolated these people are. They don't know what they're missing in the world, and they are uncontaminated by it.

Steve Estrada

It used to surprise me that the same people came back to visit the ranch. I thought that there must be something they really like here. They give their hearts for everything here, and they really want to be part of the people.

José Mondragón

The youth brushed tears from their eyes and went out into the village. The group that went to the school found that much had changed there since the previous year. The teacher had resigned, and the Honduran children, like children anywhere, took full advantage of their substitute. The atmosphere was chaotic. Four boys on the outside wanted to join in the crafts and singing, but Honduras Outreach allows only children who are enrolled in school to participate in its school events. So after school each day, the boys lay in wait and grabbed the coloring or crafts from other children and destroyed them.

Parents in the Agalta Valley didn't value education, and their children reflected that attitude, José Mondragón said. "They never needed to go to school to survive, so why should they encourage their kids to go to school? If a person completed elementary school, it did not change his way of living one bit."

José knew, however, that education was vital to the transformation of the valley. "Education is to me something like the oxygen of our existence," he told Honduras Outreach board members whenever they visited the ranch.

With encouragement from the board he devised a plan to coax parents to keep children in school. Without any announcement, he took three North American young women to six different villages to do kindergarten work for a week. The result was the same in each village. "The first day, the women worked with the children, and several people came just to see what was going on," José said. "The women talked about the importance of hygiene, brushing teeth, and other things, and they played with the children. The second day, the children came because they loved to play with the beautiful gringas. The third day, two or three kids took a shower and combed their hair. But the fourth and fifth days, all the children came nice and clean.

"Keeping children clean had not been a custom for the parents before. But the kids wanted to look nice when they were together at the school, and they asked their parents to help them do it. This is when we knew that an education project should be started. We learned that the children are the best resources we could use to change people's attitude and let them help themselves to improve their quality of life."

Honduras Outreach wanted to improve education by opening a new elementary school in the church and community center that North Americans and Hondurans had built in San Martín. The school would replace the one-room schools of thirteen villages between San Esteban and Gualaco. But the people of San Martín refused to allow their church to be used as a school.

With no building and no land, the board regrouped. "What about the money raised by the two Hands to Honduras auctions?" someone asked.

The board asked Jennifer Davis if she thought a new school would be a good use of the money, and she loved the idea. The people of Culuco agreed and donated land for the school. The central location was perfect for the children, and visibility on the main road from Juticalpa to the coast might inspire other communities to seek quality education for their children.

Honduran volunteers then completed construction, and the school was ready to open near the end of 2000. The Honduran

Years before José Mondragón characterized education as "the oxygen of our existence," Honduras Outreach had created a scholarship program to keep students in school beyond the elementary grades.

In 1993 HOI supporters funded scholarships for fifteen students to attend high school in San Esteban or Gualaco. Because the high schools were too far from the Agalta Valley to reach every day, the students received room and board with a family in town as part of the scholarship.

By 2005 there were one hundred seventy-five students on HOI scholarships. Sponsors donate six hundred dollars annually, which pays for tuition and testing fees, school supplies, room and board, and a school uniform.

While attending school the recipients do service projects such as

school year runs from February to October, so the timing was perfect. The money from the auctions was enough to provide materials and labor to build the school and pay salaries for teachers for several years. The final decision was what to name the school. Jennifer and the board wanted to honor the commitment made by members of the United Methodist Church, without making it appear to be a "Methodist school." Jennifer suggested Aldersgate, which was the place of new life for John Wesley, founder of Methodism.

When Sue explained the significance of the name to José, he suggested that the school's Spanish name be Puerta del Renacimiento, which means Door of Rebirth.

Along with the name of the school on the side of the building, the people of Culuco painted Proverbs 22:6: "Train a child in the way he should go, and when he is old he will not turn from it" (NIV). The Scripture and the school name appear

reforestation projects, neighborhood cleanup, playground repair, or abstinence training in elementary schools. Through the years some scholarship students have gone on to become teachers, health promoters, and members of the Rancho el Paraiso staff.

Scholarship recipients are selected based on their academic ability and financial status by a committee of Honduran educators along with Mirian Diaz, of the ranch staff.

Since the opening of the schools in Culuco, the scholarship program has been expanded to include elementary and middle school students in Culuco. Sponsors are assigned a student, just like the high school scholarship program, and their two hundred fifty-dollar donation supports teacher salaries and other expenses at the schools.

in both Spanish and English.

When the doors opened, many children who had not attended school for several years enrolled to get in on the excitement. Before the school opened in Culuco, sixty or seventy children at most were in village schools. Now 195 children enroll in the elementary school every year, and in 2004 there were 225. Most children receive no help with their studies from their parents, who had little or no schooling themselves. And there remains a constant shortage of books for pleasure and practice reading. But more than ever, parents are encouraging, even demanding, their children to do well in school.

Visitors who are out near the school in the early morning or midafternoon see children walking to or from Culuco wearing navy pants or plaid skirts with bright white shirts—their school uniforms. At home the children change back into their tattered play clothes, then wash their school clothes in a washtub and

Honduran parents don't generally play with their children. Men play soccer with the boys, but they play on the same level whether they are five years old or twenty. If the men are out there, the kids might as well watch out. But otherwise, you don't see them playing together.

After the North Georgia youth had worked in Culuco for three years, the Honduran parents and children presented the story of Joshua at the closing ceremony. They used props to build the walls of Jericho, then all the parents and children marched around together playing make-believe trumpets and shouting, and when the walls came tumbling down they all laughed together. It was such fun to see that huge transformation as they played with their children.

Sue Church

hang them on a barbed-wire fence to dry.

The people now see education as a way to get a better life. They're not looking to get better jobs; they will continue to be farmers and live in the valley. But with an education they can live longer and healthier. They learn to be more productive and healthier farmers.

The middle school across the road from Puerta del Renacimiento may be the clearest evidence of the people's growing commitment to education. As children completed elementary school, parents did not want their education to stop. Honduras Outreach offered them the plan for a middle school, but left it to the community to raise money for land. José never recruited volunteers. "The people made a plan, raised the money, and purchased the land," he says. "Right after we marked out the building and were ready to dig footers, people came from everywhere to help. The first day we had fifty-five men from nine communities working.

They have made their own work calendar and given themselves their own assignments."

The middle school opened in 2002, and the community named it *Esperanza*, Hope, because through education they have hope in the future. In addition to math, social studies, art, science, civics, and Spanish, students learn carpentry, cooking, farming, and other skills that will help them become self-sufficient. There is even a computer lab to assist in learning. Electricity is provided by generators since Culuco still does not have public electrical service.

"It is a very slow process," José says, "but we are now starting to see people regarding education as a tool to help make their lives easier and more interesting."

SPIRITUAL TRANSFORMATION

While the schools were being built, the spiritual training component of the ranch faced a challenge. After leading the Bible Training Center for two years, Douglas González fell ill and could not continue, and a search for his replacement began. As happens so many times with Honduras Outreach, God's call was heard and answered.

Chris Hudson, who served as summer group coordinator in 1993 and honeymooned with Monica in the hacienda a year later, often reflected on his times at Rancho el Paraiso. Chris and Monica, who is a nurse, had both experienced calls to international Christian ministry as teenagers, but the right opportunity did not arise during the early years of their marriage. Then in 2001, they decided it was time to make something happen.

They began to pray and to look into different missions organizations and were leaning toward Honduras, Spain, or Mexico.

DOUGLAS GONZÁLEZ

Edgardo Guevara sat on the front porch of his green cinder block home with Chris Hudson, who translated, and three HOI board members, Randy Mahaffey, Scott Luttrell, and Sue Church. Randy, Scott, and Sue asked questions, and Chris translated.

How do you build a congregation here?

"I do it biblically. But more than anything, we concentrate on personal relationships with people. We accomplish this through personal evangelism, going to people's homes, and visiting."

Do members support the church financially?

"At most churches in the area, almost all of the tithe goes to the pastor. I own a tile-making company, and I own a chainsaw that I rent out, so I don't receive any salary from the church. I use almost all of the tithes and offerings for others in the community."

Do you support other congregations?

"We don't have transportation, but we are beginning work in Santa

Chris felt a strong pull toward rural areas, so he and Monica decided to set up a mission trip to Honduras and see if their eyes might be opened to possibilities.

"I found an old address book that I hadn't looked at in nine years, and I looked up Jerry Eickhoff to see if Honduras Outreach was still in existence," Chris recalls. "Hurricane Mitch had hit there after our visit, and I was almost afraid the ranch might not even exist anymore."

It was a Saturday afternoon when Chris called Jerry, who told him how much HOI had grown. Fifty groups a year were going down, and pastors from nearby villages were participating in the Bible training program. "My ears perked up when he said that." Chris says. "I told him we were interested in full-time mission work, and he told me to call Sue Church."

Chris planned to call Sue on Monday, but on Sunday morning his telephone rang. "Jerry was calling back to tell me to call Sue right away. The ranch chaplain had decided to leave for health reasons, and Jerry said, 'We may have a job for you.'"

CHRIS AND MONICA HUDSON WITH ETHAN AND KATE

Chris called Sue and scheduled a trip down. Monica was pregnant, so she couldn't go.

"I was overwhelmed by the growth of the ranch," Chris says. "There were new buildings and bridges and programs, and the interaction of the groups was the ideal way to do a ministry."

The Louise Mahaffey Bible Training Center at the ranch was the clincher. In addition to his master's in divinity degree and serving as a pastor for seven years, Chris was a certified teacher. His qualifications and his calling suited the position perfectly. Convinced that God was calling them to Honduras, Chris and Monica accepted the offer from HOI. They sold their home and car and most of their possessions and moved to the ranch in 2002.

Chris led local pastors through the curriculum at the Bible Training Center. The nine members of his first class at the Bible Center represented half a dozen denominations, including Church of Christ, Mennonite, Holiness, Baptist, and Church of God.

Anna, about a half-hour walk from here. I speak there every Monday."

What is the weekly schedule at your church?

"We have a home Bible study on Tuesday afternoon and regular worship service on Thursday and Saturday afternoons. We have Sunday school every Sunday morning and an occasional Sunday evening service."

Do teachers allow prayer in schools?

"Teachers want their students to pray with them. They also sing songs and study the Bible. Teachers ask me to come to school and talk to the kids about God and the Bible. I get involved all the time. The schools have been very open to my teaching both students and teachers."

Describe a typical worship service.

"In my church we do not have a set liturgy. We are trying to avoid falling into a routine. We are always trying to modify the way we do worship. But there is singing and praising God, along with prayer and a Bible-based message that I deliver."

BIBLE TRAINING CENTER GRADUATES

"I try not to go too deep into the differences among the denominations," he says. "Instead I talk to them about basic Christian doctrine."

In a country where deep divisions exist between some Protestants and Catholics, Chris sought common ground in the love of Christ. Groups visiting the ranch saw the results on Thursday nights when they came together with staff members for worship in the dining hall. At the close of the service, all joined hands to sing and pray together.

Most pastors at the Bible Center come from villages where North American groups work. The students live in a dorm at the ranch every other week for eight months while they are studying. In addition to the classroom work, they also become involved in Honduras Outreach efforts. "We're not just helping them become better preachers," Chris says. "They're becoming village leaders promoting health and educational opportunities. They serve as an extension of the ranch in their villages."

CHURCH AND BIBLE CENTER DORMITORY

In 2004 the church across from the medical clinic was remodeled, and a new dorm for Bible Center students was built next to it so that when people from all across the valley come for medical treatment, they see their pastors committing themselves to learning more about Christ so they can carry on the transformation.

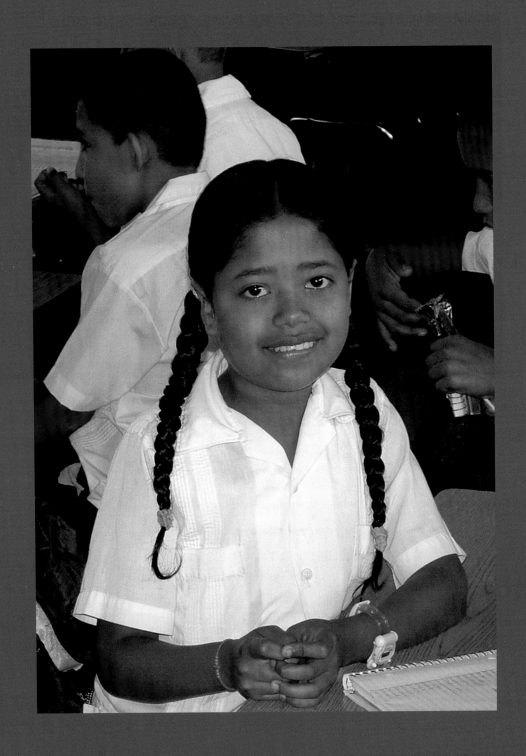

CHAPTER 14

HOPE AND A FUTURE

"For I know the plans I have for you," declares the LORD, "plans to prosper you and not to harm you, plans to give you hope and a future."

Jeremiah 29:11 (NIV)

SUCCESS WILL be measured when Honduras Outreach leaves the Agalta Valley and the local people stand without the aid of North Americans. Economic independence remains a distant but attainable goal, closely linked with education, health, medical, and agricultural programs.

One of the greatest challenges for Honduras Outreach has been teaching commercial skills to people who have no tradition of a cash economy. Atlanta public relations professional Bob Hope leads a diverse group of business people to the ranch each year to investigate and assess opportunities for commerce among the local people.

From the outset, HOI leadership has shown farmers how to raise crops and livestock to take to market, and in subsequent years villagers have sold coffee, pottery, and artwork with mixed success. Several individuals and a few villages offer rays of hope.

Reverend Gerald Varner, who spends much of his spare time in his woodworking shop, taught some of the people in the village

of El Aquacate how to use a coping saw to make wooden Christian symbols for a chrismon tree. The people used stencils to draw patterns on the wood, then held the wood with a brace while they cut it out. Gerald wished they could do more intricate work, but without electricity for power tools, it wasn't possible.

Then he saw an advertisement in a woodworking magazine for a conversation piece—a replica scroll saw driven by a foot pedal like those used in the nineteenth century. Gerald believed this was an opportunity to change the fortunes of the Honduran village. He ordered the pedal-driven saw, which turned out to be more for show than for work. But with some minor adaptations, he created a functioning scroll saw. He took it down on his next trip, along with some patterns, and taught several people in El Aquacate how to use it. Soon they were creating crosses and other pieces that they sold to North American groups in the

EUGENIO

store at Rancho el Paraiso for one or two dollars each. Convinced that the saws would work, Gerald ordered one for each of the woodworkers.

Gerald and woodworkers from other North American groups, impressed with the work of the villagers, brought more intricate patterns, and soon the people were making crosses with eighty or more inside cuts that they sold for ten dollars. North American visitors began ordering crosses and other pieces for gifts, and now the nine woodworkers of El Aquacate work almost full-time to meet demand. The sales allow them to earn almost double the average annual income of individuals in the Agalta Valley.

No one has been more affected by Gerald's commitment than Eugenio. When Sue Church met him, Eugenio was covered with bedsores from the cowhide bed he had been lying on for weeks. He had been shot in the back and was paralyzed from

the waist down. No one in the village of El Aquacate knew what to do for him. Sue, a physical therapist, talked with Eugenio's family about skin care and other needs. As it happened, Dr. Mike Priebe was scheduled to come down with his church group in two weeks. Sue contacted Mike, who brought a wheelchair and other equipment Eugenio needed.

Able to get around in the wheelchair, Eugenio still had no way to earn a living except, perhaps, woodworking. Unable to pump the foot pedal on the scroll saw, Eugenio attached a broken shovel handle to turn the drive wheel with one hand while holding the wood to be cut with his other hand. Now Eugenio is the most prolific woodworker in the village. And El Aquacate is one of the cleanest, healthiest villages in the Agalta Valley.

TWO entrepreneurial families work under the bridge over Rio de Mataderos making concrete blocks for their biggest customer, Honduras Outreach. For every latrine it builds, Honduras Outreach buys eighty blocks. At five hundred latrines annually, that's forty thousand blocks. Eight kindergartens per year require seven hundred fifty blocks each, adding another six thousand. A new house requires twenty-five hundred blocks, and room additions plus additional projects add to the demand.

HOI pays five limperas per block—which adds up to the equivalent of about $10,000 a year to each block-making family. From that amount the family businesses buy cement for sixty-five limperas a bag and pay workers one hundred limperas a day to dig sand out of the river bottom.

The margins aren't great, but the families earn more money than most of their neighbors.

HONDURAS Outreach has sought other commercial opportunities for the people of the Agalta Valley and has worked with FAMA (*Fundacion para el Apoyo a la Microempresa*) to make microloans available people in the Agalta Valley. One entrepreneur who took advantage of a loan was Rosa, who lives in Las Delicias. She has a solar cell that her sister gave her and borrowed $50 to buy a refrigerator. Now she sells cold Coca-Colas, homemade popsicles, and candy to her neighbors—primarily children coming home from school—for a few limperas.

One farmer who had been working for twenty limperas (about eighty cents) a day borrowed money for a pump to irrigate a field of Oriental eggplants that he sells for export to the United States. "Paraiso has provided an education for my children and helped me learn to grow the eggplants," he says. "The only problem is finding a market for my crops."

Although success with commerce has been spotty, the ranch staff continues to push their neighbors toward greater independence, loaning money for seeds, for example, rather than giving away seeds. The wisdom of insisting on loans rather than giveaways was evident many times through the years, especially in the wake of Hurricane Mitch in 1998.

POTTERY WOMEN OF LAS DELICIAS

Honduran people believe God is working in this place. Before Honduras Outreach there was no way for their children to go to school. And there are many other things you can see here that were not here before. The way people interact, the way people treat other people, it's all different since Honduras Outreach. The people here know it is a plan of God.

José Mondragón

Daniel walked to the ranch from his home in Cerro Chele, a trip that would have taken two hours by vehicle, to greet eight HOI board members and friends who had come down five weeks after Mitch. After greeting with smiles and hugs, the North Americans asked how his village was faring after the storm. Daniel said that their immediate needs were being met, but without help they would starve.

"The river washed away all of our crops and the topsoil," he explained. "We cannot plant a crop this season, and if someone does not help us, we will starve."

Dozens of villages in the river valleys like Cerro Chele were in the same predicament. November is planting season, but the fields that weren't washed away were still knee-deep in mud. An entire growing season would be lost to a subsistence population. Without help, thousands more in addition to the people of Cerro Chele would starve.

Several charitable organizations created seed and fertilizer
giveaway programs for the people of Honduras so that they
could plant in spring. Honduras Outreach stuck by its decision to
sell, not give, seed for crops. And this time they raised the bar
another notch, bringing two agricultural technicians and two
agronomists—all of them Hondurans—to the ranch to teach
farmers techniques for reclaiming the land and getting the greatest harvest. Farmers were required to attend the classes before
they could buy seeds and fertilizer on credit.

Two hundred fifty families in the Agalta Valley participated in
the program, and throughout the growing season they were visited by the ag technicians and agronomists, who offered further
guidance and support.

Sue Church visited several farms that summer, and at two
adjacent farms—one planted in free seed and one in borrowed

DRYING COFFEE

seed—she was followed through the field by a little dog. "In the free-seed field," she says, "you could see that dog everywhere he went. But when we crossed over into the field where the farmer had borrowed seed and gone to class, all you could see was his tail sticking up above the bean plants."

At the end of the season, only five of the two hundred fifty families had not raised a successful crop, and about 70 percent of the farmers repaid their loans.

"When you realize that these people were not even familiar with the concept of a loan," Sue says, "we were pleased that so many people paid. And the people of Cerro Chele tell others with pride that they are responsible for the credit program."

THE thing many Hondurans do best is grow coffee, but finding a market for Honduran coffee has proved challenging. Competition from large growers around the world has pushed prices so low, Honduran farmers cannot feed their families on the income from coffee. "Coffee is something good for the economy and for the environment," José Mondragón says. "Coffee needs the shade of trees in the mountains to grow best. If people fail in producing coffee because of the low price, I also fear that the forest will be cut down for lumber."

Classes and support from Rancho el Paraiso help farmers grow organic coffee, which is finding a growing market in the United States. Organic coffee requires tremendous patience, however. The crop cannot have any chemicals, fertilizers, or insecticides for five years before it can be certified. Many growers cannot wait that long. Once they have a product, the growers must then deal with coffee brokers, who are notorious for pressuring growers as hard as possible to increase production.

"THE PLANS I HAVE TO PROSPER YOU"

The greatest success of Honduras Outreach may be the ability of the people to recognize their own opportunities and problems and develop their own solutions. Year by year they rely less on North Americans for answers.

A generation of their children has received education, and they now expect their own children to advance even further in school. Dozens of villages and hundreds of homes are cleaner, healthier, and safer, and the people who live there are keeping them that way. God is doing a mighty act in the Agalta Valley through the people living there and the North Americans who come for a brief season.

God continues to call more North Americans to be His hands and feet in Honduras, to pray for the people, and to support them monetarily. He may be calling you!

After ten years as executive director, Sue Church retired in 2004, but she couldn't leave Honduras Outreach altogether. She continues to serve on the board of directors and guides the model village program that was her inspiration, traveling to Honduras at least twice a year. She was not comfortable seeing the entrance to the ranch named Avenida Sue Church, but everyone else in the organization was.

CHAPTER 15

A WEEK IN PARAISO

Many are asking, "Who can show us any good?" Let the light of your face shine upon us, O Lord. You have filled my heart with greater joy than when their grain and new wine abound.

Psalm 4:6-7 (NIV)

MAUD TYLER stood before the congregation in 1991 after returning home from her second trip to Rancho el Paraiso. She had helped build the milking barn a year earlier, and now she was home after helping to build the first dorm at the ranch.

"If you go to Honduras," she said from the pulpit, "your life will never quite be the same again. I truly feel I have left a part of my heart back there in a valley surrounded by the mountains."

It is a message repeated week after week as teams return home and report their experiences to their churches.

"We cried in our hearts at the poverty we saw in the villages," Maud continued. "We laughed with the children when they jumped and squealed at the soap bubbles we blew for them. And we embraced with love as we sat with the villagers in church.

"We loved the laughing brown-eyed people living in a land so vastly different from lands that we know. And we hated the sadness of poverty unthinkable in our eyes."

ISMAEL

Then she remembered the scene in the city of Tegucigalpa the night before the group got on their plane back to the United States. "Two tiny children in a cardboard box in a plaza after nine o'clock at night were just sitting there," she said, "and the dinner we had just eaten felt uncomfortable in our stomachs."

Yes, after a week in Honduras, your life is never quite the same again.

The change begins on your approach to Tegucigalpa near midday on Saturday, as you look out the airplane windows at deep brown scars cutting through the green mountains—mudslides from Hurricane Mitch, reminders of the devastating 1998 storm. The plane banks sharply over the sprawling capital city, giving you a bird's-eye view of desperate poverty—rows and rows of shacks clinging to steep hillsides, and you wonder how they will survive the next storm.

One more sharp turn and the pilot has lined up with the runway. Automobile traffic has been stopped on the highway below because the plane must come in low to allow for a quick stop on the short runway. (Stoplights were added to keep the highway clear a few years ago after the landing gear of a jet nicked a passenger bus below.) Then the wheels hit the runway, the pilot throws the reverse thrusters, the plane screeches to a stop, passengers applaud the pilot, and God hears their prayers of thanksgiving.

The doors open, and the North Americans step into 1950. Stairs have been rolled over to the plane, and they climb down to the tarmac and enter one of the smallest international airports in the world. A smiling Honduras Outreach group leader meets the North Americans near the customs area and helps get their bags to the bus for the ride out of the city.

The ride through Tegucigalpa gives the visitors a closer look at the wretched poverty that grips almost every inhabitant. Close up, the "houses," many scrabbled together with scavenged materials, look even more vulnerable than from the air. Many of

the people look tattered and tired. But there is a frenetic busy-ness to the city as well, as cars and bicycle riders squeeze through narrow streets, and crowds mill among sidewalk markets. Outside the city center the bus stops for fuel at a Texaco station, and visitors buy cold Coca-Colas like they remember—made with pure cane sugar instead of high fructose corn syrup.

Down the backside of the mountains that ring the city, the bus passes people digging along the roadside. They are collecting limestone, which they will grind and sell or use themselves, mixing it with cornmeal before making tortillas. It is one of the few sources of calcium in the Honduran diet.

An hour or so out of Tegucigalpa, the bus pulls over at the Wayside, a Mennonite bakery, for fresh-baked banana bread, coconut candy, and other treats. Then it's back onto the bus and on to Juticalpa, the capital of Olancho, where the group will spend Saturday night.

HOI EXECUTIVE DIRECTOR BETH BARNWELL

The streets of the small city are narrow, dusty, and almost deserted compared with Tegucigalpa. In the center of town is a hard-packed park with sidewalk vendors, some old, some young, some eager, some quiet, outside the cathedral across the street. And in a field across from the hotel on any given night, there is soccer.

ON Sunday morning it's on to the ranch. After stopping for gas and a stretch at the DIPSA station, the bus turns north off the paved road. Any conversations from here on will have to be yelled; the only moments of quiet are bridge crossings.

The group arrives at the ranch at about eleven in the morning, unpacks, then settles in briefly before lunch. Many groups then load up and ride out to visit the village where they will be working. Few among the North Americans speak Spanish, and usually none of the villagers speaks English. But the smiles and

ROSA

MIRAN DIAZ AND CARLITO

laughter communicate genuine love for one another. They will spend the next three and a half days working side by side.

The work is hard and the heat relentless. The most common task for North Americans is mixing concrete, also known as "doing the crater dance." After mixing seventy shovelfuls of sand with a eighty-pound bag of cement, they create a volcano shape, pour water into the crater, and mix. While construction teams are working on homes, another team teaches Bible school to the children of the village.

In the evening the teams return to the ranch exhausted, thankful that North American-style dormitories with running water and comfortable beds, and long porches with rocking chairs and hammocks await. Dusk turns to night, a peace that can only be experienced, not described, envelopes the ranch.

At four o'clock the next morning, the kitchen crew arrives and begins preparing breakfast for the visitors and staff. By the end of the week the North Americans will have eaten a year's worth of

JOSÉ AND ELENA MONDRAGÓN
WITH MELLIE AND FRANCISCO

beans and tortillas. The staff complements the staples with fresh fruit and vegetables, eggs or pancakes for breakfast, and beef, chicken, or fish for lunch and dinner.

The rooster crows, and the group rises, gets dressed, and gathers at the foot of the cross. Another day in Paraiso.

By Thursday afternoon the work in the village is complete and the bonds of friendship are as strong as the mortar in the joints. North Americans and Hondurans celebrate their work with songs, prayers, and hugs. In years past, your group leader might have taken you up to a nearby waterfall high in the mountains on Thursday afternoon. The water has since been diverted, however, to generate electricity for the valley.

On Friday, it's time to leave the valley. As you leave you look around the bus and realize you have built stronger bonds with your fellow travelers as well. You have traveled to the mountaintop with them.

RANCH STAFF SOCCER TEAM

LUCAS

"We found a time to know and love each other," Maud Tyler told the congregation. "The members of our group cared for each other, were tender and interested in each other's thoughts and feelings, and a very special glow of heart warmth enveloped us all.

"Then the long bumpy bus ride through the beautiful mountains and the lowlands was over," she continued. "Our time in the hot noisy city of Tegucigalpa had passed. And finally we were on the plane bound for home. As it started to take off I closed my eyes. I thought of these and many other memories, and for a few moments I wondered, *Did our work really help these people?* I hammered nails in a cow barn. Can that make a difference?

"Then an old phrase entered my mind: 'O God, my boat is so small and the sea is so wide.'

"Again I saw in my mind the waterfall we had visited after climbing a mountain late one hot afternoon. As the cool water rushed downward, the sun shining through the leaves caused

MARTA

rainbows to dance in the water in both the bright and the dark corners of the river. And I remembered also the rainbow that shyly appeared over the ranch early on the morning of our departure. And I knew that our God, their God, in His time and with the use of many human hands, brings rainbows of a better life for these warm and loving people."

BY ARCHIE CRENSHAW

A CITY ON A HILL

God is not a secret to be kept. We're going public with this, as public as a city on a hill. If I make you light-bearers, you don't think I'm going to hide you under a bucket, do you? I'm putting you on a light stand. Now that I've put you there on a hilltop, on a light stand—shine!

Matthew 5:14–16 (The Message)

WHEN YOU boil theology to its essence, the mission of the church is to go into all the world and to preach the word of God to every creature, and then to do good to other people. "I was hungry, and you gave me food. I was thirsty and you gave me drink. I was a stranger and you took me in" (Matthew 25:35).

Those kinds of things are what Honduras Outreach is all about. It's not always a sermon. It's simply the presence of Rancho el Paraiso. The ranch is a great lighthouse. It's a city set on a hill. I have grown to appreciate that a lot more. I've seen so many unbelievable things happen there, and there are so many stories we don't know about.

When we started providing scholarships for children to attend school, I happened to be at the ranch the day that applications would be available. It's amazing how the people around the ranch don't have any communications network, but somehow news

gets out by word of mouth, travels like wildfire, and people came in from everywhere.

This particular morning when I woke up, there must have been two hundred people gathered around outside the hacienda for applications. One old gentleman who had lost a leg and had just a peg had walked all night to get an application for his grandson.

The people of the Agalta Valley see light, leaven, and salt. They see Christianity in action. They see Jesus living through the lives of the people who go down there. Even as we get involved in things as "nonchurchy" as commerce, it's unbelievable what will happen. We will lend a lady one hundred dollars for a sewing machine, then she'll learn to sew, and it will change her life. We will make a small loan so a farmer can buy a pump to irrigate an acre of crops, and his gratitude overflows.

I find that I am less religious and more spiritual than I have ever been as result of these and other experiences in Honduras. That's nothing to boast about. If the apostle Paul wrote today, he would say, "I am chief among sinners, but Crenshaw over there is worse than me." But right now I have best the relationship with the Lord that I have ever had. I am so grateful for that.

Jesus has been introduced to people in Honduras in a very favorable way, and souls have been saved. Many North Americans, while helping the people of Honduras, have also invited Christ into their lives. We often bring back more Christians than we take down, and the light of the world glows brighter in North America.

Honduras Outreach, Inc.
Decatur, Georgia
(404) 378-0919
HOI.org
E-mail ASKHOI@hoi.org

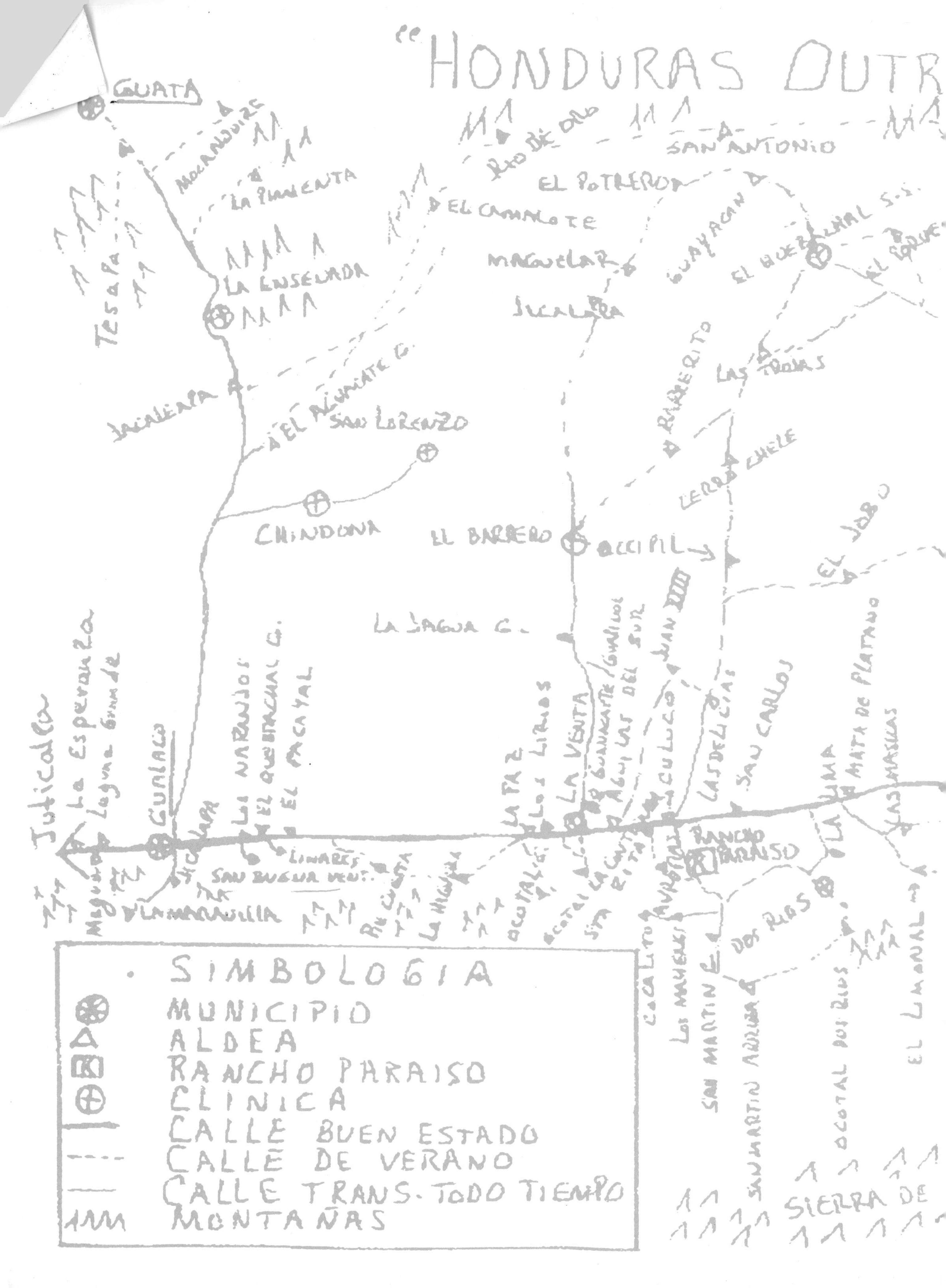

GUATA

MOLANDURE
LA PIMENTA
TESAPA
LA ENSELADA
JACALEAPA

RIO DE ORO
SAN ANTONIO
EL POTRERO
EL CAMALOTE
MANGUELARES
JICALAPA

GUAYACAN
EL QUEBRACHAL S.L.
EL SQUE...
BARREQUITO
LAS TROJAS

A EL ALMIATE G.
SAN LORENZO
CERRO CHELE

CHINDONA
EL BARRERO
OCOPIL
EL JOBO

LA SAGUA G.

Juticalpa
La Esperanza
Laguna Grande
Guayaco
ACHUAPA
LA NARANJOS
EL QUEBRACHAL G.
EL MACAYAL
Mayala

LA PAZ
LOS LIBROS
LA VENTA
GUANACASTE
AGUA CALIENTE
GUAIJIQUIL
JUAN XIII
LAS DEL SUR
CULUCO
LAS DELICIAS
SAN CARLOS
LA LIMA
MATA DE PLATANO
LAS MASIAS

VILLANUEVA
LIMARES
SAN BUENA VENT.
BUENA VISTA
LA HIGUERA
OCOTALES
OCOTAL
STA
OCALITO
LOS MANUELES
AVERDAL
RANCHO PARAISO
DOS RIOS
OCOTAL DOS RIOS
EL LLANAL
SAN MARTIN
SAN MARTIN ARRIBA
SIERRA DE

· SIMBOLOGIA

⊗	MUNICIPIO
△	ALDEA
⊠	RANCHO PARAISO
⊕	CLINICA
——	CALLE BUEN ESTADO
- - -	CALLE DE VERANO
——	CALLE TRANS. TODO TIEMPO
⌒⌒⌒	MONTAÑAS